Social Work: A Very Short Introduction

VERY SHORT INTRODUCTIONS are for anyone wanting a stimulating and accessible way into a new subject. They are written by experts, and have been translated into more than 40 different languages.

The series began in 1995, and now covers a wide variety of topics in every discipline. The VSI library now contains over 350 volumes—a Very Short Introduction to everything from Psychology and Philosophy of Science to American History and Relativity—and continues to grow in every subject area.

Very Short Introductions available now:

Available soon:

For more information visit our website

www.oup.com/vsi/

Sally Holland and Jonathan Scourfield

SOCIAL WORK

A Very Short Introduction

OXFORD
UNIVERSITY PRESS

Great Clarendon Street, Oxford, OX2 6DP,
United Kingdom

Oxford University Press is a department of the University of Oxford.
It furthers the University's objective of excellence in research, scholarship,
and education by publishing worldwide. Oxford is a registered trade mark of
Oxford University Press in the UK and in certain other countries

Published in the United States of America by Oxford University Press
198 Madison Avenue, New York, NY 10016, United States of America

British Library Cataloguing in Publication Data

Data available

Library of Congress Control Number: 2014959009

ISBN 978–0–19–870845–2

Printed in Great Britain by
Ashford Colour Press Ltd, Gosport, Hampshire

Contents

List of illustrations

Chapter 1
What is social work?

The troubled teenage boy who cannot settle in a foster home; the frail older woman who is desperate for social contact; the community seeking a way to tackle gang violence; and the disputed territory of international adoption. The man with serious mental health problems who is facing homelessness; the parents struggling to cope with their children, who are also causing problems in school; the rural village in Africa with no clean water supply; the teenage girl caught up in an exploitative relationship with an older man.

A group-based programme designed to help men who are abusing women to change their behaviour; the care arrangements which allow a very ill older man to stay in his own home as long as possible; the meeting of wider family members to decide where the children of drug dependent parents are going to live, because they cannot safely stay where they are. Supporting an impoverished community in setting up a micro-finance system for small businesses; negotiating with the local housing department to arrange a move and a fresh start for a family who are harassing their neighbours; advocating for a young person with learning disabilities to secure supported work.

All of this is the territory of social work. Its variety makes it fascinating but also poses a challenge in pinning down what exactly makes it distinctive and where its boundaries lie.

Definitions

Defining social work is pretty difficult. Debates rage about what its main aims should be and what kinds of activities count as social work. The first two chapters of this book cover this terrain. Chapter 2 introduces some of the main fault lines of debate about what social workers should be concentrating on. This first chapter deals with definitions, history, and boundaries.

A short working definition is that social work is a community-based response to social need. We did not make that up but borrowed it from an advert for a lectureship. The university social science school which was seeking the new staff member wanted to use the broadest possible definition in order to maximize the field of applicants in an academic area which has not traditionally attracted too many top researchers. Our general stance in this book is that broad is good in defining social work.

A broad definition is necessary of course when looking at any social phenomenon internationally because of political and cultural variations. But even within a single country, breadth is needed in defining the thing because the boundaries are very blurred, as we shall see in this chapter. 'Social need' is included in the short definition because social workers spend their time trying to ease social suffering. They encounter the extreme casualties of social inequality: the victims of poverty, illness, addiction, and abuse (as well as abusers). They operate in the space between the state and the poor or marginalized.

Another possible short definition is that social workers help people improve their social functioning. It is the person in their social environment that social workers attempt to influence. Many of the people social workers help have personal troubles, but it is how these troubles link to the social environment that is the business of social workers. By social environment, we mean people's relationships with family members, friends, and fellow neighbourhood residents; we mean their dealings with social institutions; we mean the wider context which affects their everyday lives—that is, their incomes and opportunities for work, cultural values within communities, the physical state of their home and the streets where they live. Social workers help people function in these contexts and that help may include trying to change those contexts, as will be seen later in this book.

There are several published attempts at a definition of social work. Harriet Bartlett wrote a well-known one in the American context in 1958. There will be many examples of definitions for specific countries, which inevitably reflect the social work role as defined by the laws of that country. The best place to start for a book which attempts to be international in its scope is the definition agreed by the International Federation of Social Workers and the International Association of Schools of Social Work. The first version of this was agreed in 2000 and a revision was published in 2014. The core definition is reproduced in Box 1. The definition is meant to make sense anywhere in the world. What we

Box 1 The new global definition of social work

Social work is a practice-based profession and an academic discipline that promotes social change and development, social cohesion, and the empowerment and liberation of people. Principles of social justice, human rights, collective responsibility, and respect for diversities are central to social work. Underpinned by theories of social work, social sciences, humanities, and indigenous knowledges, social work engages people and structures to address life challenges and enhance well-being.

Agreed by the International Federation of Social Workers and the International Association of Schools of Social Work in July 2014.

immediately notice is the ambitious rhetoric of empowerment, liberation, and social justice. These powerful words reflect social work's tradition of aspiring to change the wider social and political arrangements that lead to people being in very difficult circumstances.

What can be challenging about this grand rhetoric is that the mundane reality of everyday practice will probably not live up to it. Maybe that is often the case for summary statements about any academic or practical discipline—a general definition is necessarily sweeping and grander than any specific example could possibly encompass. But there is perhaps a particular problem of social work realities being a long way removed from aspirational talk of social justice. It is not that social justice is not relevant to social work. But whether social work can really achieve social justice is more debatable. One risk of having grand rhetoric is that the lack of fit with the everyday makes social workers feel that they can never do enough.

The Secretary General of the International Federation of Social Workers, Rory Truell, contrasts the 2014 definition with one from 1957 he found in the Federation's archives:

> Social work is a systematic way of helping individuals and groups towards better adaptation to society. The social worker will work together with clients to develop their inner resources and he will mobilise, if necessary, outside facilities for assistance to bring about changes in the environment. Thus, social work tries to contribute towards greater harmony in society. As in other professions social work is based on specialised knowledge, certain principles and skills.

This definition is very different from the 2014 one. It uses the masculine pronoun, as was common practice at the time, even though most social workers are women. It is markedly different in being based on the preservation of the existing social order rather than social change. We can see the influences of the historical roots of social work in both the older and newer definitions, so this is a good point to turn to history.

Social work's history

It is not possible here to provide a full history of social work but we simply highlight a few important themes. The first is to note that there has been a gradual move over time in most countries towards more secular state provision. Social work has tended to grow out of charitable works and many social workers are still employed in charitable organizations. In the early days of social work many organizations or individuals were religiously inspired. However, the 20th century saw the state moving into provision of a safety net for the most vulnerable people in society. Welfare state regimes were established and took over responsibility to provide for social need. Secular social support came to be provided as a right under the law rather than through the good works of religious folk.

This is the story in capitalist countries at least. Communist countries have seen a rather different pattern, with a period of silence about social work while the existence of social problems and the need for additional support for the casualties of these problems were denied on the grounds that there were universal basic services under state socialism. During the period of silence, services did not progress and humanize in the same way as in the capitalist West, as can be seen vividly in the terrible state of the orphanages in Eastern European countries that were opened up to scrutiny in the early 1990s. In more recent years, there has been a rebirth of social work in Eastern Europe and the fairly rapid setting up of systems to train practitioners.

In Africa and Asia, postcolonial countries have pursued social development alongside infrastructural development. This would include activities ranging from residential homes for orphans to grass-roots education to prevent violence against women and girls. The term 'social work' would be used less often than 'social development'. In countries which have rapidly industrialized, such as Japan, Taiwan, and Korea, the development of social work is fairly recent and influenced by international precedents. Social work could be used to mitigate the side effects of social change brought about by rapid industrialization (e.g. in Korea).

A shameful aspect of social work's history can be seen in the fate of the Aboriginal population of Australia. The 'stolen generations' are Aboriginal children who were taken from their families, ostensibly in the interests of social welfare (see Box 2). In contemporary times, social work in Australia is still mostly run by the white majority, but there is increasing respect for indigenous knowledge and the idea that this knowledge could be a basis for social work practice which is more legitimate in its cultural context than Western social science, which usually provides the underpinning theory and evidence for social work (see Chapter 6).

Box 2 The stolen generations: a shameful period in social work's history

Between the late 19th century and the 1970s very large numbers of Aboriginal and Torres Strait Islander children were taken from their families and placed either in institutions or in white Australian homes. This happened in the apparent interests of social welfare, with these children thought to be at risk. Indigenous models of child-rearing did not fit the European template, and assimilation was an unquestioned goal of social policy. The result was the separation of children from their birth language and culture. In retrospect the practice is considered a scandal, and was the subject of an official apology by Australian Prime Minster Kevin Rudd in 2008.

In contrast to this history of cultural imperialism, contemporary social work is more likely emphasize the importance of ethics, progressive values, and the promotion of human rights, as seen in the 'new global definition' (Box 1). 'Anti-discriminatory' and 'anti-oppressive' practices have been espoused by social work writers, meaning that practice should tackle the effects of discrimination on the grounds of someone's identity: gender, 'race', religion, sexual identity, and age. Commentators have questioned to what extent everyday practice lives up to this ambitious rhetoric, especially when social workers employed by the state tend to have to work within narrow bureaucratic limits and with limited funds to support people. However, it should be noted that the mainstream social work approach in the 21st century is to respect and value cultural and social diversity.

There are some divergent historical roots which have merged in contemporary social work but could still be said to be causing tensions in defining its role and purpose. We are referring in particular to the Charity Organization Societies and the Settlement movement. The former originated in the UK but had equivalents in other countries. In the UK the Charity Organization Society (COS) was set up in 1869 as an initiative to combat idleness in the poor. It was established to help the poorest people in 19th-century Britain to avoid dependence on charity by teaching them self-reliance based on scientific knowledge. This was the beginning of assessment and casework, with charity members visiting families to judge how deserving they were of support and give advice on managing a home.

In contrast, the Settlement movement was based on students from universities and private schools going into impoverished areas to set up facilities for communities. The social gap between worker and service recipient was perhaps no less than with COS, but the emphasis was on community-wide help rather than the identification of needy and deserving individuals. Famous settlements were Toynbee Hall in East London and Hull House in

Chicago. Hull House, for example, ran community resources such as art and literary education and sports clubs, with a particular emphasis on helping poor immigrants to adjust to American society. A photograph of 'a gypsy boy in the games room' can be seen in Figure 1. Hull House was also politically influential, lobbying for change on a range of issues. It was involved in setting up the first public playground in Chicago and campaigning to desegregate the Chicago public schools. Hull House was set up by social work pioneer Jane Addams who won the Nobel Peace Prize, and two of the original buildings now form a museum.

The different emphases of COS and the settlements on reforming individuals and reforming society can be seen in the differences between the 1957 and 2014 international definitions. They can also still be seen in contemporary debates about social work's purpose, which we will discuss in more depth in Chapter 2. We

1. Photograph from Hull House. 'A gypsy boy in the game room'.

return to aspects of social work's history at various points throughout the book, and to the settlement movement in more detail in Chapter 5.

Most countries where social work has a recognizable identity have gradually moved over time towards professionalization. This has involved increasing expectations of educational achievement and regulation of the boundaries of social work. Only certain types of training will be recognized as suitable preparation, and membership of a professional body might be a prerequisite to claiming the title 'social worker'. The ideal of a 'profession' as distinct from other occupations can be understood in a number of different ways. A positive take on the term is to emphasize a unique expertise and public service ethos. A more critical stance is to see the process of professionalization as maximizing the status of a small group and excluding others—a form of occupational 'closure'.

A unique problem that social work has with professionalization is that for some people a distinctive element of social work philosophy is eschewing professional expertise but instead promoting the perspective of the 'service user' or 'client' (see Chapter 2 on terminology). For various reasons, social work has struggled to gain professional status. Reasons include the contested (disputed) nature of expertise, the lack of a clear boundaried knowledge base, and the lack of consensus about methods. It has also been argued that there is a gender inequality dimension to this issue and that in comparison with high-status, traditionally male-dominated professions such as medicine and law, social work and nursing—both fields mainly staffed by women—have been branded 'semi-professions'.

This brings us to our final theme in relation to social work's history—that of gender. Most of the pioneers of social work are women and the workforce is dominated by women. Helping people with personal troubles is a feminized activity; that is, some of the qualities required for this type of helping, such as being a good listener and having empathy, are among the socially constructed characteristics of women. (By 'socially constructed' we mean characteristics that are created by society, rather than being rooted in biology). Caring is regarded as something that women are good at. Commentators have also noted that where social work is a relatively low-status job men are not attracted to it, and as in many professions there is an over-representation of men in senior management roles.

A gendered aspect which is less often highlighted is that most of those who receive services from social workers are women. This can be understood in similar terms to the over-representation of women in the workforce, namely that within families it is traditionally seen as a woman's role to sort out personal troubles. Thus in child and family social work there is a particular problem of women as mothers being expected to take responsibility for behaviour change when the role of a man in the family may in fact be the biggest problem that needs to be addressed. It does not have to be this way and there has been some interesting development of approaches to work with men in various countries. However, this does remain something of a Cinderella area within social work.

What distinguishes social work from other professions?

The knowledge base of social work is contested, which causes a fundamental problem with defining social work and drawing conceptual boundaries around it. Although some claim social work is a separate academic discipline, it is probably best described as an interdisciplinary field which relies heavily on various academic disciplines from social science, and most obviously on sociology, psychology, and political science.

Within this range of influences there is no clear consensus on what constitutes the right mix. Older, more established professions such as medicine and law have a fairly high level of internal agreement about core knowledge and the principles that should guide the selection of relevant evidence for practice. Some of the internal debates within social work are outlined in Chapter 2. At this point we consider how social work is distinctive from some other professional fields concerned with personal and/or social functioning with which there could be considerable overlap.

As noted at the beginning of this chapter, we favour a broad interpretation of the term. This is going against the trend in our own country (the UK) where, despite emerging differences between England, Scotland, Wales, and Northern Ireland, the historical trend has been a move towards an ever more specific definition, focused narrowly on the statutory social work role.

The UK working definition has narrowed to the extent that Charlotte Drury, a Cardiff doctoral candidate doing an ethnographic study of child welfare, recently found a voluntary sector family support team stressing that what they did was 'not social work', in order to differentiate themselves from the perceived deficits of the statutory social workers who client families lived in fear of. This was despite the fact that the relationship-based work they were doing was completely in tune with traditional approaches to social work help for families.

Broader conceptions of social work are more familiar from other countries. In the United States, university schools of social work encompass much of what in the UK would be termed social policy and also work on aspects of public health.

Public health

Public health is the first field we will consider in terms of its similarities to and differences from social work. Contemporary public health improvement programmes frequently include social interventions. In recent years, there has been increasing emphasis within the public health field on socio-ecological models which, rather than seeing health behaviours as the sole responsibility of individuals, take seriously the impact on people's health of local cultures, socio-economic context, and national laws and policies. This sounds like social work to us. A socio-ecological approach may be more novel in a field which is essentially a branch of medicine, but it is bread-and-butter conceptual background for social workers and has a much longer history within social work.

An example of a social intervention offered under the umbrella of public health is the provision of parenting courses which demonstrate respectful techniques for managing children's behaviour that are more effective and humane than physical chastisement. This would seem to be traditional social work, falling somewhere in between advice-oriented casework and community-level provision. However, in our experience in the UK these courses are not often facilitated by social workers and they are more likely to be claimed by public health.

There are differences between public health and social work. The former tends to emphasize population-level universal interventions, and social work has never been universally provided but has always existed for those in greatest need. Targeting services for people in need is something that some public health professionals and researchers would be positively suspicious of, as targeting itself can cause problems, with the risk that the label of 'need' or 'problem' might become a self-fulfilling prophecy.

Another difference is that the public health field is obviously strongly informed by a medical model, whereas social work has a more ambivalent relationship with mainstream medical model approaches. In practice, many social workers work closely with medical staff and accept mainstream medical diagnoses and treatment regimes. However, there is a more critical tradition, with social workers drawn to approaches which are quite anti-medical, such as the social model of disability which sees society as the cause of disability rather than the impaired body (see Chapter 2) and anti-psychiatry critiques from people who have received mental health services. Yet another difference is that the public health field is much more supportive of a scientific model of evidence-based practice. As will be explained in Chapter 6, the social work field is more resistant to this.

To sum up, public health could be said to have recently stolen some of social work's clothes in its use of a socio-ecological model, but there are obvious differences from social work, such as the close relationship with medicine, widespread application of scientific evidence, and a tendency to take a more universal approach to population health, as opposed to targeting services on need.

Counselling, psychotherapy, and community psychology

Counselling and psychological interventions are part of the social work role in many parts of the world and are quite compatible with social work, but are not synonymous with it. Essentially, they are concerned with individual psychological functioning, while social work, being concerned with the person-in-environment, has to be broader. Breadth is one of social work's strengths but also a potential weakness, as breadth inevitably means lack of depth, leading to the perception that social workers know a little about a wider range of different kinds of help but are not experts in any one kind.

Social workers do use counselling skills, and share with counsellors Carl Rogers' ethic of unconditional positive regard for clients. The Barclay Report of 1982, which set out to define social work in the UK, included counselling as a core social work task, but only alongside work at the community level, not in isolation from it. Whereas social work can claim to be the originator of social interventions that are used in other professional fields, it clearly cannot claim to have invented counselling, which has a history of its own.

Social work has drawn heavily on psychology for as long as that discipline has existed. Psychology itself is a highly differentiated discipline. Although the use of scientific method is mainstream, there are fringes of psychology which are more influenced by critical qualitative social science (i.e. sceptical about measurement and using research approaches that are closer to the humanities than to science). There is also the rather separate tradition of psychoanalysis which has been very influential in social work, with Freudian assumptions being widespread among practitioners during the latter half of the 20th century. It is still very common to encounter social work teams talking of repressed past trauma coming to the surface in 'acting out' behaviour, and the need for troubled people to be encouraged to talk about the root cause of their difficulties in childhood. In Chapter 2 we discuss the debates about the value of this approach.

The term 'psychotherapy' is usually used to refer to any talking therapy which is based on psychological theory. Many kinds of psychotherapy are drawn upon in mainstream social work practice. Behaviourism has been influential, and now the wider family of cognitive-behavioural approaches is used in some fields. Social workers tend not to deliver what clinical psychologists would recognize as pure psychotherapy, but rather they would more typically adapt approaches within routine casework relationships.

It is perhaps helpful to provide a brief example of the distinction between psychological approaches and social work. If a middle-aged man ('Joe') with an alcohol problem was allocated a social worker he might expect counselling which uses motivational interviewing skills, a subtle behaviour change technique from psychology, or perhaps help to gradually change his drinking patterns using a drinking diary—a behaviour modification approach based on social learning theory. So far this is all psychology. However, if the social worker's initial assessment includes the wider context of Joe's social relationships and she encourages him to build his social capital (i.e. productive relationship networks) through volunteering with a local youth charity and helps to mediate his difficult relationship with his daughter, this ceases to be just counselling or psychotherapy. It may be that the counselling element would not be as intensive as that offered by a dedicated counsellor, but the social worker would be using counselling skills and knowledge of psychological skills as *part* of a broader approach to helping. James Barber's book *Social Work with Addictions* does a good job of conceptualizing a distinctive social work approach.

A branch of psychology which shares social work's focus on the person-in-environment, and the importance of changing the environment as well as the individual, is community psychology. There is considerable commonality between the two traditions, but they have developed separately. Community psychology is the relative newcomer, and is a much smaller field than social work.

Community development

A field which has developed a separate identity from social work in some countries, but could be seen to be integral to it, is community development or community organizing. This involves working with people to help them improve the quality of life in their communities. A broad definition of 'community' can be used, to include communities of interest or identity as well as those based on geography (see Box 3). This is the settlement tradition within social work, and it is the main focus of Chapter 5.

Those who work in this field and see themselves as in a separate category from social work might not agree with our position, but we see community development as having grown out of social work. A separate identity perhaps only evolved because social work was trying to straddle both a community-based approach and a more individualized focus. In the UK, as noted earlier, social work in the public sector has become very heavily focused on individual

> **Box 3 Support for service users to self-organize**
>
> Offering logistical support to a group of people who are disabled or have mental health problems in order to help them set up and run their own support service—is this social work? There is a possible paradox here because the setting up of such a service might do some social workers out of a job, as the emphasis shifts away from the need for professional assessment and management of care. However, this is very much in keeping with the community development tradition of social work and also the more recent tradition of promoting the expertise of service users.

casework and high-risk situations, so to look for opportunities for a community focus you need to look to the non-governmental sector.

The community development tradition in social work places emphasis on community self-organization, with workers providing some professional support to community members but following their agenda rather than leading it. There is a tradition of political action, with community groups being supported in lobbying for policy changes and for better provision of services. Community education was an important aspect of the original settlements, but this has evolved quite separately in many countries, being provided within education services rather than social services.

Allied to community development is the social development tradition, emerging from countries of the Global South. The priorities of social development tend to be different from those of social work in the Global North, if it takes place in countries which do not have the government funds to finance generous welfare state provision. Social work cannot claim social development as its own, but there is considerable overlap and many social workers work within social development.

There are other professional categories which have some similarities with social work but are not synonymous with it. The term 'human services' tends to refer to the administration and management of social services, rather than to the direct face-to-face practice which is the domain of social work. 'Youth work' refers to social intervention with young people, but it is usually limited to informal education and support rather than intervening with all aspects of a young person's social circumstances. In the UK there is a broader term 'social care' which encompasses all social support, including informal care in families, and is distinguished from the narrower 'social work' which in the UK is the domain of qualified practitioners. In light of the field's global diversity, in this book we keep the scope of 'social work' broader than just what is done by those with a formal social work qualification.

It should be remembered that the kinds of professional boundaries discussed in this chapter do not necessarily matter to people receiving services. Social workers may be preoccupied with professional identity or status, but their clients are much more likely to value good-quality relationships, reliable workers, and forms of help which are effective in achieving their aims.

This chapter has struggled with the vexed question of what social work is. It is perhaps surprisingly difficult to answer this question, because social work has emerged from contrasting traditions which overlap with other domains of helping, and because it does not have a well-boundaried knowledge base. The rest of the book will take up the themes raised in this introductory chapter.

Chapter 2
The politics of social work

Social work is inherently political because its parameters are set by the government of the day, and many social workers are employed by the state and have important legal powers through that employment. Debates rage about social work's purpose and methods, so the field is also highly political in the sense of this OED definition of politics: 'the assumptions or principles relating to or underlying any activity, theory, or attitude, especially when concerned with questions of power and status in a society'. This chapter covers both aspects. The bulk of the chapter deals with some of the big debates about the purpose of social work, its assumptions, and principles or values. A final, shorter section focuses on the relationship between social work and government.

The politics of practice

Various attempts have been made to come up with a framework which fits all the different approaches to social work. David Howe's 'taxonomy' of theories has been influential. Its categories are the 'fixers', who use expert knowledge to help individuals to adjust to society; the 'seekers after meaning', who use individualized client-centred approaches; the 'raisers of consciousness', who are concerned with inequality in society but aim for personal control more than political change; and the 'revolutionaries', whose aims are to change society rather than the individual, perhaps through the application of Marxism or radical feminism to social work.

One way in which Howe's taxonomy could be criticized is in its lumping together contrasting approaches into single categories. For example, the 'fixers' include both behaviourist approaches and psychodynamic approaches which are at odds with each other (see the section on 'Understanding the past vs practical help with present functioning'). Malcolm Payne's framework takes these criticisms into account. He identifies these three overarching views of social work:

- Reflexive-therapeutic
- Social order (individualist-reformist)
- Transformational (socialist-collectivist)

These can be represented diagrammatically, with any social work practice positioned according to how it relates to each of the three views (see Figure 2). Rather than illustrating these three headings at this point, we will highlight the range of views about what social work is for, where social workers should target their efforts, and what methods they should use, by outlining four big debates in the field.

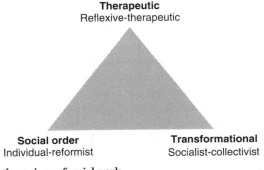

Therapeutic
Reflexive-therapeutic

Social order
Individual-reformist

Transformational
Socialist-collectivist

2. **The three views of social work.**

Individual problems vs social conditions

Few if any social workers would disagree that the social circumstances of their clients are strongly implicated in the problems they experience. Few would dissent from the idea that better income and housing would go some way to ameliorating these problems. However, there is less agreement about the extent to which social workers should target their efforts on individual problems or social conditions.

In the 1970s, some workers influenced by Marxism started to argue for 'radical social work'. They were motivated by a critique of mainstream practice that saw help for individuals as fairly pointless, as this was simply a sticking plaster for the wounds of inequality caused by capitalism. A magazine was set up in the UK called *Case Con*, punning on the familiar social work institution of the case conference. Casework with a few people in extreme need was thought to be the wrong approach, and what was needed instead was to work with communities to campaign for political change that would ease social suffering for the larger group of people living in similarly challenging circumstances. The idea was that casework's emphasis on change in the individual who is experiencing difficulties ends up blaming that individual for problems caused by an oppressive society.

Others would argue that this approach is based on an overly optimistic view of family life and underestimates the extent of personal problems and oppressive relationships. Children and adults need to be protected from abuse and neglect and this requires casework. There is an inevitable balance to be struck between care and control, and quite rightly some people need to be helped to adjust to social norms: for example, in the case of a teenage boy whose anti-social behaviour is causing mayhem for other working-class residents of the estate where he lives—to work on his behaviour is simply being socially responsible.

It could be said that promoting behaviour change is just taking inequality seriously. If we regard many personal problems as having their roots in social inequalities rather than individual pathology, then to help people with those personal problems which are the symptoms of inequality is part of the process of combating inequality. It could be said that the effects of inequality cut very deep, and simply to improve someone's housing, as the result of a social work-supported local campaign on that issue, will not necessarily improve their relationships with partners and children in the short term. If someone has learned a parenting style which prevents them forming a close attachment to their children because of their own experience of emotional deprivation in childhood, then a bit more money and a nicer house may not immediately lead to big changes in parenting style. They may also need help to change the parenting itself, and to be shown how to talk to children in ways which build better relationships. Equally, to only focus on parenting tasks, as if parenting occurs in isolation, and not to tackle environmental pressures could be very unhelpful. An exclusive focus on individual behaviour could be seen as not actually social work at all, if social work requires attention to the person-in-environment.

Perhaps the best that social workers can do is to help their clients improve their quality of life, even if only in a small way, via some kind of social intervention. This may have some socio-political implications—e.g. you can think of helping an abused woman to leave a violent man in terms of the wider picture of gender relations—but it is not in itself political change.

The social worker might be able to go a bit further and make the case for more refuges or better policing or a new intervention for perpetrators, or they might even help set some of these changes in motion, but that is as much change as they are likely to achieve. The larger structures of inequality will remain unchanged, and to really change these structures you ultimately need governmental action. That might be achievable through lobbying or it might mean trying to get a different political party elected. And, indeed, many social workers draw on their everyday knowledge of social inequalities to take part in political campaigning. But inevitably social and political change requires more than social work practice on the ground can ever deliver on its own.

Understanding the past vs practical help with present functioning

Within the array of approaches to casework there are some very different emphases, and some of these can clash with each other. Chapter 3 provides a proper introduction to casework with individuals and families. The aim at this point in the book is simply to highlight one fault line in the casework approach, that between past and present.

Let us take an example of Mike, a man in his thirties who is depressed and struggling to cope with his children, often losing his temper. Mike's childhood was unhappy and he still has an up-and-down relationship with his parents. In adulthood he has lost a close friend to suicide.

A psychodynamic social worker, working in a broadly Freudian tradition, might argue for exploring the roots of Mike's depression in his childhood and his experience of bereavement. The idea here would be that only understanding and coming to terms with past trauma will improve Mike's mental health in the present; he needs 'insight' into the root causes of his difficulties. The appropriate intervention from this perspective would be talking therapy based on an intensive relationship with a social worker (as represented by Clare in Figure 3), although in some countries this would be arranged with a specialist therapist rather than directly provided by the social worker.

In contrast to this emphasis on the past, a social worker with a cognitive-behavioural bent would deliberately focus on present

3. Clare in the community.

behaviour. She might decide that dwelling on past trauma
would only risk deepening Mike's self-defeating beliefs that are
maintaining his depressed state. Instead, this social worker would
offer Mike help in modifying the negative thoughts which
underpin his depression, and also advice on different parenting
strategies which would improve his management of his children's
behaviour without resort to shouting and ineffective punishments
doled out in anger. Again it may not be the social worker herself
who would provide this help. In some countries she would and in
others she would 'refer' Mike to get this help from a specialist
service. This could be individual therapy for depression and
attendance at a parenting programme such as Incredible Years,
which is based on social learning theory and teaches parents
about the importance of praise, warmth, and consistency in
childcare.

Because they are social workers, rather than clinical psychologists,
both the psychodynamic and the cognitive-behavioural social
workers should also provide material help and probably case
management (Chapter 3). However, there are real differences
between their approaches which cannot be skated over in an
attempt to broker a compromise 'eclectic' approach. They cannot
both be equally right. Proponents of psychodynamic work would
argue that cognitive-behavioural approaches only scratch the surface
and do not lead to longer-term changes. Cognitive-behavioural
adherents would, however, argue that only their approach has a

meaningful evidence base (see Chapter 6), and that even small changes in thinking and behaviour can lead to big differences in quality of life for all concerned (Mike's children and partner as well as himself).

Intervention vs non-intervention

Although social work would seem to be a humane response to social need, it cannot in fact be assumed that intervention is always helpful. The high point of optimism about social work and its wider role in civilizing society can be found in the writings of sociologist Paul Halmos. His articles and books set out a vision of society in which a broad category of personal service professions, in which he includes doctors, nurses, and teachers as well as social workers, have a positive influence on the whole of society through their moral leadership. Their care ethos, emerging from Christianity and social science, could have a profound and positive effect by moderating competitiveness. This is how he put it at the end of his article 'The personal service society' in 1967. In using the term 'professionalization' he includes the crucial influence of the personal service professions.

> I believe that professionalization in the capitalist west inevitably introduces more and more collectivistic and other-regarding considerations into social functioning, and weakens the laissez faire licence of a free enterprise, the rapacity of penal justice, the harshness of educational discipline and the mercenariness of 'marketable' doctoring. (p. 27)

In sharp contrast to this optimism about the humane influence of social work and other people-oriented professions, is the idea that sometimes the best approach is *non*-intervention. Sociologist Edwin Schur coined the phrase 'radical non-intervention'. We have particularly seen this in relation to young offenders, where the dominant practice at the end of the last century (in the UK at least) was to avoid bringing them into the criminal justice system at all costs, so they would not become labelled as deviant. This approach was strongly informed by labelling theory from sociology: the idea that identifying someone as deviant can lead to that deviancy becoming exacerbated, with the individual themselves and people around them starting to interpret their behaviour in line with the label. Young people mixing with other offenders in prison can obviously exacerbate offending if the other inmates are identified with. But even social work supervision might have the effect of labelling a young person as an offender, and therefore it was avoided unless absolutely necessary.

We see debate about the virtues of intervention in all the fields of social work. We have mentioned parenting help a few times already. It might be thought to be benign because parents value it and the evidence is good in terms of outcomes for children. However, some critics see the expansion of early intervention in families as part of surveillance creep, with everyday parenting becoming ever more scrutinized.

Debates rage about whether or not we should be taking more children into care or fewer. The UK government elected in 2011 took the line that adoption is good and there should be quicker decisions about taking children away from parents who are really struggling to provide appropriate care and are unlikely to change. Others are critical of any increase in numbers of children coming into care, seeing this as a failure of the state to offer adequate help in preventing family problems. These critics tend to emphasize the socio-economic dimension, with the children of the poorest people being disproportionately more likely to be taken from their parents. This is perhaps not so much a debate about whether there should be intervention or not as a fundamental disagreement about what kind of intervention is appropriate—should taking children into care be something we try and avoid or something we embrace as a positive decision?

Medical model vs social model

The fourth fault line is that between social and medical approaches. Many social workers work in medical settings or alongside doctors and nurses in multidisciplinary teams. Yet there is a strong social work tradition of critical distance from a medical world view.

Many social workers around the world feel comfortable in supporting medical care. In the US there is a strong tradition of social work in health care settings, with terms such as medical social work and clinical social work being widely used. Such social workers would not necessarily experience a clash of values with medical colleagues, but would see themselves as providing distinctive services such as family meetings, arranging practical help in the home after discharge, or counselling for victims of abuse.

However, not all social workers are so comfortable with a medical model, and not all would see a biomedical approach to people as conducive to the progressive aims of social work. In particular, there have been strong critiques of mainstream medicine in relation to disability and mental health. A powerful critique, from some disabled people's organizations and some disabled academics, has been that the medical model of disability sees disability as located in the flawed body of the individual. In contrast, a social model of disability turns this around and sees society as disabling people with impairments (e.g. limitations of mobility or vision) through the barriers it puts up. These barriers include the inaccessibility of places (e.g. buildings) and social opportunities (e.g. mainstream education and jobs) to people with impairments. The health and care professions are themselves implicated as disabling because they have set up specialist services for disabled people only, keeping them segregated from mainstream provision.

One implication of this critique is that disabled people themselves should be centrally involved in the design and delivery of services as well as making decisions themselves about their care. There has been a movement in some countries towards care (or 'support', to use the term that some disabled people's organizations prefer) which is managed by the user of the service—that is, the person receiving the support is in control of the money that is spent on the support. This calls into question the need for a social worker to assess and coordinate care. However, in countries where the social model of disability has influenced policy, social workers have often argued in favour of this approach. It is in keeping with a strong trend in contemporary social work of prioritizing the voices of people who receive services.

In the mental health field there has been a similar challenging of medical approaches, with some patient groups being critical of mainstream psychiatry and its reliance on biological explanations for illness and pharmacological treatments. Some social workers have been very sympathetic with this critique, themselves favouring explanations for mental health problems that root them in social circumstances (abuse, poverty), and preferring social interventions such as supporting people to find employment and building up social networks.

There are counter-arguments. In the mental health field, recent scientific advances suggest there are in fact important biological causes of mental illness. It is also the case that very many people feel positive overall with the medication that makes their illness manageable and would not take an anti-psychiatry stance. In relation to disability, there have been calls (e.g. from British disabled academic Tom Shakespeare) to break down the unhelpful dichotomy of medical-social, because although social arrangements are vital to the quality of life of disabled people, so is medical care. And as noted earlier, most social workers in practice work in support of medicine rather than in opposition to it.

It could be argued that lobbying for a social understanding of health, illness, and disability, and for appropriate social interventions as well as medical treatment, has meant that in many countries these positions have moved into the medical mainstream. It is routine in mental health for medical professionals to claim to be using a 'bio-psycho-social' approach. So groups of patients and service users, as well as social workers, could in turn claim to have had some influence on medicine, although pressure for change has also come from within the medical profession. The downside of this for social work is that once the mainstream accepts the importance of a social perspective, and health care professionals try to provide help with social difficulties, the need for a distinctive group of workers to provide a social perspective could easily diminish.

What do we call the people we work with?

We end this discussion of debates within social work by mentioning the various views concerning what to call the people who receive social work services. There is not so much a clear fault line between two opposing arguments as a range of views.

Different opinions to some extent map on to differing views about whether or not social workers are experts. In many settings, people are simply described by a social category such as 'parents' or 'young people', and this would be fairly uncontroversial. It becomes trickier when attempting to give a general description of people who have social work contact.

It is sometimes necessary to use a shorthand for this diverse group of people. 'Clients' is probably the term most often used in the majority of countries. However, there are objections around to this term. Some argue that it does not describe people who have not chosen to have a social worker but have had one allocated by the state. The idea of a professional relationship entered into freely does not capture their situation. Others object to 'client' for a very different reason, namely that it implies professional expertise such as that offered by lawyers and accountants, whereas social workers should be led by the expertise of the 'client' themselves.

Some prefer the term 'service user'. This has become the politically correct term in the UK, though it may have negative connotations in other countries. It could be seen as a neutral term which does not imply any particular power relations. It is, however, far from elegant and some dislike the term on that basis. Others have seen it as implying a consumerist relationship with services which may or may not exist. Yet others are happy to embrace this implication, to the extent that they favour the term 'consumer'.

Finally, to recognize the expertise in their own circumstances that is held by social work service users, some have argued for the term 'experts by experience'. In this book we use a range of terms, but we are quite content with 'client' as it is respectful and recognizes that social workers do (or should) have some social scientific expertise.

Social work and government

There is considerable international variation in the relationship between social work and the state. In some countries, social services are provided almost exclusively by charities. In others, the ownership of social work has evolved over time to a situation where most social work services are now run by local or national government organizations. Some countries also have a thriving private sector where social work is one of a range of services run for profit.

The relationship of social work to the state depends in part on the welfare state regime of the country. Danish sociologist Gøsta Esping-Andersen's book *The Three Worlds of Welfare Capitalism* describes the differences between welfare states in affluent

'Western' countries, using three broad categories of liberal, corporatist-statist, and social democratic.

Liberal regimes are found in, for example, the United States, Canada, and Australia. They are mainly characterized by the dominance of the market and private provision, with the state only getting involved to meet the very most basic needs. Corporatist-statist regimes include France, Germany, Italy, and Spain. In these countries, social assistance is based on contributions made through insurance schemes and there is an emphasis on family preservation. Social democratic regimes can be found in the Nordic countries, where there is a strong emphasis on universalism and social protection against inequalities caused by the market, with the state taking direct responsibility for individuals.

In most affluent countries in particular, social workers have some powers invested in them by the state. These might include, for example, powers to intervene to protect children or remove them from their parents' care, assess adults who may be vulnerable to abuse or neglect, and take part in the process of compulsory admission to a psychiatric hospital.

To expand on the last of these and give an example, the Mental Health Act 1983, which applies to England and Wales, included the role of 'approved social worker', which has more recently become amended to 'approved mental health professional' (AMHP), with this person not necessarily having a social work qualification. An AMHP's agreement is required alongside that of a psychiatrist before someone can be compulsorily admitted to hospital for the sake of their own health, safety, or the protection of others. This is recognition in law of the value of a social perspective on the patient's well-being. Where social workers have far-reaching statutory powers such as this, they have a clear control function and cannot be described simply as advocates for clients. Social workers need to have a good understanding of relevant laws. This might mean knowing about more than one level of legislation—for example state and federal levels in some countries.

Having a statutory responsibility to protect means that social workers can be under intense pressure from public scrutiny. In the child protection arena in particular, social workers can feel as though they are criticized whatever stance they take. Decisions to leave a child in a high-risk situation or take a child from its parents are equally likely to be vilified in the press if questionable in hindsight. It has been described as a 'damned if we do, damned if we don't' dilemma.

In some countries, policies in relation to social work have been driven by scandal (see Box 4). Ian Butler and Mark Drakeford have described this process in the UK over the last fifty years in their book *Scandal, Social Policy and Social Welfare*. Not only have scandals arisen about child protection, but also regarding the

Box 4 The 'Baby P' scandal

In 2008 a child protection failure scandal hit the British press. A seventeen-month-old baby, at that time anonymous but later identified as Peter Connelly, had been killed, most likely by his mother's boyfriend. The local authority, Haringey in North London, had been under the spotlight several years earlier because of another notorious child death, that of Victoria Climbié. A media storm followed and the tabloid newspaper *The Sun* started a campaign to remove the Head of Children's Services in Haringey, Sharon Shoesmith. She was the senior manager responsible for child protection in the area and she had apparently refused to apologize or resign. The government minister responsible, Ed Balls, took the highly unusual step of announcing her sacking in parliament. She has since won a case for unfair dismissal and received a six-figure sum in compensation.

poor-quality care of people with learning disabilities and mental health problems. Responding to a scandal does not necessarily lead to good policies that are based on evidence and taking a long view of what is needed.

Although many social workers are employed by the state, therefore sometimes giving them limited room for manoeuvre in voicing critical opinions, there is a certain tradition of challenging government when needed. Social workers' activism is usually informed by their particularly close-up view of the negative consequences of government actions or inactions. Some social work organizations, particularly those in the non-governmental sector, engage in lobbying about particular issues they encounter. An example would be women's refuge organizations, which might lobby local and national government about better services and better policies to prevent domestic abuse. As noted earlier, some would argue that this dimension of political activism is essential to the core of a profession whose aim is social justice.

Social work is suffused with politics. Even if not employed by the state, social workers operate within government policy, though they might also campaign to change policies if they are having a detrimental effect on their clients' lives. So, if you like, Politics with a big P is a crucial backdrop to understanding the social work role. But perhaps more important is what is sometimes referred to as 'small p' politics, namely that there are debates to be had and decisions made about the big ideas—such questions as what should social workers be spending their time doing? Is helping vulnerable individuals missing the point when their vulnerability is caused by social injustice? Is it even helpful for a person to have a social worker if this fact teaches him that he is a problem? Are mainstream social work services disabling? And what kind of help leads to behaviour change—is it learning insights into the roots of your difficulties, or practical measures which make it easier to do some things you couldn't do before?

These debates and others will surface at various times during the rest of the book. The next three chapters—the core of book—are divided up according to the target of social work help, with separate chapters on work with individuals and families (Chapter 3), work with groups (Chapter 4), and work with communities (Chapter 5).

Chapter 3
Social work with individuals and families

Introduction

Much professional social work practice is carried out with individuals and their families. This is particularly true for professionals employed by the state, in the Global North, and in urban, industrialized countries. There are a number of shared features in much of this work. First, most social workers will wish to attend to the person's social context rather than only the specific problem being presented—who looks after them and who do they look after; do they have enough money, shelter, and food to meet their basic needs; what are their arrangements for health care and do they have any other problems? Second, most social workers also aim to work in a manner that is relationship-based. This means they recognize that the developing relationship between the social worker and client can itself be part of the helping process because it is easier to talk about problems and work towards solutions with someone you have come to trust. Thirdly, it is generally accepted that a strengths-based model—where the practitioner recognizes and attempts to bolster a person's strengths as well as respond to their difficulties—is an approach that fits with social work's value base and produces a more productive working relationship.

Origins

There is a long history of social work with individuals and families. Here we concentrate on two early texts because they express so well some of the enduring aspects of casework in social work. In terms of the modern profession, Mary Richmond's book *Social Diagnosis*, published in the US in 1917, set a standard for a systematic, planned approach for social workers to gather and analyse evidence and put in place plans to alleviate social problems (see Figure 4). Richmond herself acknowledges that there are historical antecedents to her methods, citing the individual inquiry work of Reverend Chalmers in his parish in Glasgow in the 1820s, and the systematizers of poor relief in Eberfeld, Germany.

Richmond declared that her social diagnosis method could be used with people experiencing all types of individual problems, including disabled people, the chronically ill, and children at risk of harm (and also, as she labels them in the spirit of her time, 'the inebriate, the insane, the feeble-minded and the unmarried mother'). Richmond supported specialization of areas of knowledge, but felt that scientific methods could be applied across a range of cases. Her advice on methods for reaching a thorough understanding of a person's situation is largely still valid today. She suggests the worker should draw on a wide number of sources of evidence, analyse that material by collating it and relating the separate parts to each other, pay attention to new information that contradicts what is thought to be known about a case, and examine strengths as well as weaknesses. In common with modern texts on social work assessment she maintains that early impressions should be treated simply as a hypothesis and that workers should hold more than one hypothesis in early stages until evidence is gathered to confirm or disconfirm each one.

Interestingly, although Richmond can be seen as attempting to turn social work into a scientific endeavour, her acknowledgement

4. Mary Richmond: a pioneer of casework with individuals and families.

of the human aspects of the work is striking. When writing about accurate diagnosis she notes that all humans are individual, and that there is a limit to how much we should categorize them. She makes a case for social workers possessing two main traits. First, they should have a good knowledge base about what social services can do in a variety of situations. Second, they should carry positive values—what she calls a 'generous conception' of 'the possibilities of human nature—of the suggestibility, improvability and supreme value of folks' (p. 376). In this, she is an early adopter of the strengths-based approach.

A second classic text, published in New York in 1964—half a century after Richmond's book—was *Casework: A Psychosocial Therapy* by Florence Hollis. This text focuses on interpersonal problems and is rooted in Freudian theories and their application to the treatment of individuals. It marks a time when there was widespread confidence in the application of Freudian psychoanalytic theory as a central feature of social work.

The book is not, however, solely about therapy. It is clearly about the social work method of casework, 'the person-in-his [*sic*]-situation' and is therefore concerned with social settings as well as individual problems. Like Mary Richmond, Hollis emphasizes that casework is both an art and a science, demanding creativity, skills, systematized knowledge, careful observation, and experimentation. Again, like Richmond, Hollis also requires practitioners to hold specific beliefs about human nature: 'They must care deeply about helping their clients, and be warmly accepting of them as they are' (p. 265). This echoes the psychologist Carl Rogers' later approach of 'unconditional positive regard' for counselling, mentioned in Chapter 1, which has been highly influential in casework and group work within the context of social work. It is an approach that might be said to have faded somewhat with the emphasis on risk assessments in many countries since the 1990s.

Contemporary organization

Almost since the inception of social work there has been some degree of specialization, with some social workers involved mainly with children and their families, while others help disabled, mentally ill, or older people, or work with offenders. Although generic social work delivery has had its moments, in recent years there has been a tendency towards even more specialism, in terms of working with specific client groups and also different stages of helping. In the UK, for example, it is common for social workers working with children and families to be organized into separate teams for receiving initial referrals; child protection; family support; children in foster, kinship, or residential care; adoption; disabled children; youth justice; and young people leaving care. This degree of specialism means that workers become experts in particular tasks and areas of knowledge, but it can mean that some families face regular changes of social worker as their needs are reassessed, or they may have many workers if they have a disabled child, a child in trouble with the law, a parent who misuses drugs, and a grandparent with dementia.

Social workers may be located in specific social services, often provided by the state through local governments. They are often located in schools, hospitals, hospices, and prisons. In a number of countries there are multidisciplinary teams, working with (for example) adults who are mentally ill, young offenders, and people needing cancer care. This has the advantage of bringing together a wide range of skills in one place for those who need help, but for social workers in particular it can lead to challenges due to the broad and sometimes fuzzy definition of their role. While a psychiatrist will clearly be engaged in medical diagnosis and clinical treatment, social workers may need to justify what they bring to the team that may be different from, for example, an occupational therapist or community psychiatric nurse. The Australian Association of Social Workers put out a position paper in 2012 that justified social workers' roles in such settings, citing:

> The unique attributes, skills and knowledge that Social Workers bring to generic and specific mental health services; for example, understanding the consumer's social situation and relevant strengths and stresses, engaging with family carers, and connecting with local services and resources.

In some industrialized nations, state-provided social work has become highly individualized, with some commentators expressing concerns that it has become a 'fire fighting' service that responds to referrals about risk and the most acute need. This results in social workers becoming case managers who assess risk and need, and refer individuals and families to other services for therapeutic interventions and practical services.

Mandatory reporting is in place in a large number of countries, including most of the United States, Canada, and Australia. This means that any member of the public (or in some states only professionals who have contact with children) must, by law, report any suspected or known child abuse. In some cases mandatory reporting also applies to vulnerable adults. Mandatory reporting has led to huge increases in referral rates for abuse. This has undoubtedly led to some children and vulnerable adults being protected from abuse who might otherwise not have been helped.

On the other hand, there are disadvantages to such legislation. In the United States, for example, fewer than a third of reports are substantiated and even fewer of those receive any form of help. In the meantime families have had to face the stigma and upset of a child protection investigation, and stretched public services have had to put precious resources into responding to every report. This has led to the development of Differential Response Systems, which allow for a less adversarial approach and allow families facing less serious allegations to be offered voluntary assessment

Box 5 High referral rates

In December 2013 Los Angeles County child protection service workers went on strike to highlight how they cannot keep children safe with the ratio of staff to referral rates and high caseloads of active cases. Around 1,600 social workers were on strike for six days, held emotive rallies, and were subject to arrests as they demanded that case load maximums should fall below thirty families per social worker.

and services, but the problem of high referral rates remains a global problem (see Box 5).

In parts of the Global North, such as the United States, social workers may offer their services in private practices. Here they are likely to be offering specialist assessments for court cases or counselling and therapy. The fees are likely to be out of the reach of people living in poverty, but may be paid by health insurance or mandated by the court. Charities—also known as voluntary sector services, the third sector, and non-government organizations (NGOs)—are also important providers worldwide. Some have their roots in religion, and the major world religions are still important providers of social services in many countries. Some suffered blows to their reputations when abuses or questionable practices of the past were uncovered, such as the coercive removal of babies from unmarried mothers, the mistreatment of children in children's homes, and the policy of transporting children from the UK far from their families of origin to Canada and Australia. Modern charities often attempt to fill the gaps left by government provision. This can lead to social work in these organizations sometimes being more innovative or specialist, although in the Global South NGOs may be providing the bulk of social welfare services.

When social workers work with individuals and their families, they are generally doing one or more of three things (see

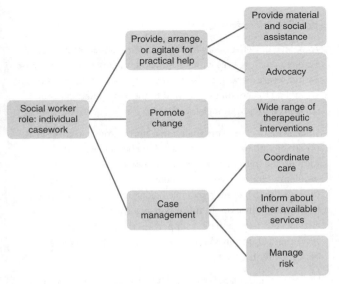

5. Social worker roles with individuals and families.

Figure 5): first, providing practical help (either directly or by helping to access resources from elsewhere); second, trying to promote or facilitate change in their attitudes, behaviour, self-beliefs, mood, or motivation; and third, case management. Case management involves assessing need and risk, making plans to assist or intervene, reviewing plans, and closing cases. With many individuals all three areas will be needed, but sometimes the focus will be narrower. Some contemporary social workers complain that they spend too much time on case management and not enough time providing practical help or promoting change.

Provide, arrange, or agitate for help and support

A core task for social work is arranging material and social help for others. For Awa (see Box 6) and her family, practical help may

Box 6 Case examples

Awa, an eighty-five-year-old migrant from Somalia to a Western European nation, lives with her son and his family. She has breast cancer, heart disease, and some memory loss. Her family are struggling to care for her safely at home. Her geriatrician has suggested they seek social work help.

Linda lives in a homeless shelter in a North American city. She is pregnant with her fifth child. All of her children live with her mother due to Linda's alcohol dependency and mental health problems. She sees her children only when supervised by a relative due to her unpredictable behaviour. She has abstained from alcohol throughout this pregnancy with the support of an alcohol counsellor and peer support group. Child protection services must decide whether her newborn baby can remain in her care after the birth.

Fifteen-year-old Adam lives in a children's home in Northern Europe. He has been in care since he was eleven when he ran away from home and reported physical abuse from his single father. He lived in five foster homes prior to coming to the children's home. He has been communicating with his father on Facebook and wishes to return home.

ease their situation and enable her to stay at home with her family. Help may come in the form of aids and adaptations to the home—such as handrails for the stairs and the bath, or even a stair lift that means she can safely access the upstairs of the home—if her ability to walk has deteriorated. A social worker may also arrange for help with Awa's care, in the form of arranging for an assistant to come to the home to help with bathing and other caring tasks. They can attempt to maximize the family's income by making sure that they claim all of the welfare benefits they are entitled to. They can also provide social support such as linking Awa and her family to support groups, and emotional support by listening to Awa and her family's feelings as they face these changed circumstances.

As Awa lives with a family who appear to be concerned about her, we might assume that her basic needs for food, shelter, and clothing are met. However, Linda, the expectant mother in the homeless shelter in North America (Box 6), will need help with these basics and will need to provide these for her baby. A social worker will have many roles with Linda, but agitating for housing and a basic income may be a first priority. In such circumstances power relations may shift, and the social worker may move from being a powerful assessor of potential risk to the baby to an ally and advocate alongside Linda, leading her through bureaucratic systems and helping her to access constrained pools of resources.

While arranging practical help and emotional support of this type can seem to be a neutral endeavour, devoid of any theory except the desire to ease suffering, many social workers will see this type of helping within a range of conceptual frameworks that fall under the loose umbrella of social justice approaches. Most users of social work services are poor, and many will additionally lack power in relation to the rest of the population or face discrimination because of other aspects of their identity, for example, because they belong to an ethnic or sexual minority, or because they are women, disabled, mentally ill, or elderly. In chapters 4 and 5 we will see that tackling structural inequalities is usually associated with group and community approaches, but many social workers believe that some of this work can be done at an individual level. As well as advocating for individuals, social workers can raise awareness of needs within local services in order to improve those services. Box 7 shows an example of social work moving authority away from professionals and facilitating families to find their own solutions to problems.

A number of theoretical positions recognize the impact of the individual's material and social circumstances on their

Box 7 Family group meetings

Family group meetings are a potentially radical form of social work with families because the method turns traditional social work practice on its head. Instead of a practitioner assessing a problem and offering a potential solution to a family, or a family being invited to attend a meeting with a large roomful of professionals who will discuss their needs and any risk they pose, the family is put at the helm.

Originating in New Zealand and drawing on Maori practices, family group meetings have been adopted across the world and used to tackle child welfare concerns primarily, but also older people's care, mental health, and substance misuse problems. Self-defined family groups are brought together and encouraged to discuss and come up with a plan for tackling the problems they face. This is likely to rally their own support networks and also draw in the professional help they think they need.

While the evidence on outcomes is somewhat mixed, there is clear evidence that this approach is popular with families *and* professionals, and can lead to unique and creative solutions to problems.

well-being. These tend to draw on sociological understandings that social structures and social practices shape life experiences and opportunities to take part in society. Those living in socio-economically disadvantaged positions—such as those on low incomes, those who are jobless, less educated, homeless, or living in poor housing, or those facing prejudice because of their gender, race, sexuality, or disability status, for example—are more likely to experience social and health difficulties. Social workers who draw on these sociological theories to inform their practice will pay attention to issues beyond individual behaviours. Social work approaches that encompass an understanding of the impact of social inequalities in society have variously been labelled anti-racist social work, anti-discriminatory practice, anti-oppressive practice, feminist social work, Marxist social work, radical social work, and critical social work.

Advocacy is an approach that recognizes that individuals requiring social work help will be relatively powerless in the social welfare system and may need help expressing their views. Advocacy has often been seen as a core social work activity, as the social worker speaks on behalf of their client. Some organizations in the UK now provide independent advocates, as it is acknowledged that it is sometimes hard for the social worker to be advocating *for* someone, while also potentially making difficult decisions that the client does not accept—for example that they are not eligible for a service, they cannot return home, or they pose a risk to other people. The advocate's role is to help express the client's wishes without adding any value judgement or further analysis.

Children and young people in care are sometimes offered advocates, as it is recognized that they may not have an adult to speak up for them and they can feel powerless. In the case of Adam, the boy who wishes to return to his father's care (Box 6), an independent advocate might be helpful because his social worker is likely to have to conduct a risk assessment of the situation (see section on 'Case management' later in this chapter) and Adam may not agree with the results.

Promote individual change

As well as the social justice approaches already described, social work with individuals and families has a strong tradition of more individual approaches. While practitioners using approaches that promote individual change may well recognize the social and economic inequalities inherent in their clients' lives, they also recognize that change at an individual level is possible and often necessary. For example, these approaches may be underpinned by an understanding that poverty is a stressor that can exacerbate substance misuse, crime, or child neglect, but their proponents may also note that not all people living in poverty have these problems.

The types of intervention discussed in this section tend to have their roots in the discipline of psychology, and are sometimes known as 'psy' approaches. They would include the work of psychodynamic theorists such as Freud, and behavioural theorists such as B. F. Skinner. Theoretically these 'psy' approaches thus cover a broad spectrum, but they have in common a desire to promote change in individuals and families through increased understanding and through learning new behaviours.

Casework based on psychodynamic approaches was the dominant social work approach in much of the Global North in the middle decades of the 20th century. Insights from theorists with a focus on parenting and children, such as John Bowlby and Donald Winnicott, emphasized the importance of the parent–child relationship, the impact of early experiences, and the trauma associated with separations. It fell out of favour as an overarching approach from the late 1960s onwards as other approaches became more popular. These included approaches based on a critique of structural inequalities, and more focused individual casework such as task-centred work and cognitive-behavioural approaches.

However, it should be noted that psychodynamic theories still have a strong influence on social work with individuals and families. For example, attachment theory based on Bowlby's work, which documented the effects of the separation of babies and their mothers in World War II and was further developed by Mary Ainsworth, continues to be an important consideration in decision making in foster care and adoption (see Box 8). The core of the theory is that our experiences of responses from our main carers lead us to form internal working models of our own self-worth, and of how people are likely to behave towards us. This working model

Box 8 Attachment theory: examples

Decision making about removing children from their parents' care in cases of child abuse and neglect is influenced by attachment theory in many Western nations. In the US and the UK in recent years there has been a policy push to remove children from abusive or neglectful parents' care as early as possible so that they can form primary attachments to new permanent carers who are either relatives (known as kinship carers), long-term foster carers, or adopters. A child's need for permanent relationships with carers may take precedence over the legal rights of birth parents. Elsewhere in Europe the legal rights of birth parents are never severed unless they give permission for adoption.

In the case of Linda (Box 6), the expectant mother whose older children are cared for by their grandmother, her social worker will place importance on the new baby's need for a secure, reliable, and permanent relationship with a primary care giver. This may be Linda, her mother, or a non-related carer such as an adopter.

When making decisions with Adam, who wishes to return to his father, his social worker may include in his or her analysis an assessment of Adam's severed relationship with his father and his difficulty in forming meaningful attachments to any of his foster carers. At fifteen, Adam may prove able to offer his own insights into this.

can be confirmed or modified according to our experiences as we develop.

Therapeutic interventions with children—such as life story work and play therapy—are influenced by psychodynamic theories, including the need for children to make sense of their early experiences in order to form positive relationships with new carers. Social workers often emphasize the importance of the relationship between themselves and their clients as therapeutic in itself, and are encouraged to be reflective about their own role in the relationship. These ideas are influenced by psychodynamic theories and may be differentiated from a more neutral, clinical approach that places most emphasis on the technique of the intervention such as in cognitive-behavioural work.

A popular approach for working with individuals and families—at least with social work students who are required to name the theoretical basis for their work—is crisis intervention theory. This theory was developed in the 1940s by US psychiatrists Gerald Caplan and Erich Lindemann, and rests on the assumption that times of crisis offer opportunities for change. Crises may help people express their feelings, recognize the need for change, and make people more willing to accept help.

In the later decades of the 20th century, a push developed for more evidence-based and purposeful forms of social work intervention to promote change in individuals. There was a concern that psychodynamic social work casework was open-ended and outcomes were difficult to measure.

The task-centred approach was developed by William Reid and Laura Epstein in the US in the 1970s. It is attractive in that it is a time-limited, structured, and transparent method that can be explained to clients. Unlike psychodynamic therapies, there is little emphasis on past experiences. Social worker and client agree on the nature of the problem and develop goals. These are broken down into small, achievable tasks. Progress is measurable.

In the early 1980s James Prochaska and Carlo DiClemente, who were researching smoking cessation, developed a theory of the stages of change in health behaviours. These are:

- Precontemplation (person is not considering any change in their behaviour)

- Contemplation (person is expressing a desire to change)
- Action (person starts to change the behaviour)
- Maintenance (person has changed lifestyle and is sustaining change)
- Relapse (this is a common feature and does not preclude the person changing again in the future)

This theoretical model has been widely applied in health and social work in areas such as drug and alcohol misuse. The model is relatively easy to explain to people with problem behaviours and helps reassure them that other people go through similar processes, including relapse. William R. Miller and Stephen Rollnick later developed a model of 'motivational interviewing', originally for people with drug and alcohol dependency. This provides social work and health professionals with specific skills to help people move from precontemplation and contemplation, through a stage of preparation for action, to behaviour change. Practitioners explore ambivalence in people's attitudes and what might help them move towards change. Linda (Box 6), the homeless mother in North America, may well have been helped on the road to recovery by social workers using motivational interviewing to engage her in changed behaviour.

Systemic and ecological approaches

For a number of decades social workers have been encouraged to consider individuals' lives within a social and ecological system. It is recognized that individual behaviours, strengths, and difficulties are heavily dependent on their social and environmental network. They live within a web of relationships of different intensity, from close family to friends, neighbours, helping professionals, colleagues, and community. Social workers may rely on this theory to assess and analyse a person's situation. For example they may map the person's social network and environment on an 'eco-map', which might look something like the map for Awa in Figure 6.

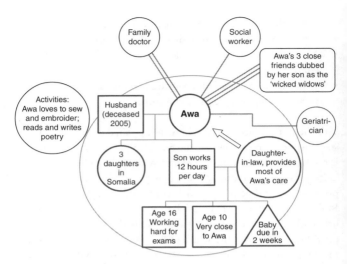

6. A simple eco-map for Awa.

Many details can be added to an eco-map, such as the relative strength and level of reciprocity of relationships (in the eco-map in Figure 6 the strength of relationships is shown by single, double, or triple lines, with a jagged line for a relationship Awa is unhappy with), geographical locations, and changes over time, such as an important person who has since died. Such a tool can quickly aid an in-depth conversation and allow a social worker to gain a sense of a person's social resources and any gaps there may be. It might be redrawn from time to time to demonstrate how, for example, a person's social support network has increased or how unwelcome parts of the network, such as those sustaining problematic drug use, have decreased.

Systems theory recognizes that the different social systems in which an individual is embedded are interconnected, and that a change in one part of the system might have an impact on other parts. This pattern of change can be unpredictable and unexpected, and is not necessarily linear.

One intervention that often rests, theoretically, on systems theory is that of family therapy. Family therapy emerged later than the development of individual psychotherapy. Therapists recognized that many individual psychological and conduct problems originated from, were aggravated by, or were sustained through relationships with others. In general, the theory proposes that a family is more than a sum of the individuals within it. While family therapists may come from a number of disciplinary backgrounds, including psychology, psychiatry, and education, many are social workers by background. The history of attention to the person-in-environment in social work fits well with systems theory and family therapy interventions.

Systems may be placed more broadly within an ecological framework, and this is sometimes referred to as ecological-systems theory. Urie Bronfenbrenner is a key social theorist in the development of ecological-systems thinking, which has a strong influence on social work and psychology. He identified the individual as being located within a series of interacting and dynamic systems. The individual is most closely connected to the *microsystem* which includes his or her family and other close relationships. The *mesosystem* is the relationship or connection between the individual and his or her family with other systems that have an immediate impact such as school, place of worship, and community facilities. The *exosystem* has an influence on the individual but at one step removed. For example, for the child, their parents' workplace will have an influence due to shift patterns, rates of pay, and perhaps stress levels. The *macrosystem* has an impact on the broader cultural and political environment, such as customs, laws, national social policies, and religious traditions. *Chronosystems* acknowledge the influence of time. This includes human development over the life course and historical time (the era in which one lives). Importantly, the ecological framework offers a very broad base for analysing individual experience, encompassing individual traits and motivations, interpersonal relationships, physical resources, and the impact of culture and social policy.

Some might argue that ecological-systems theory is most useful for understanding a person's situation and less useful for determining a course of action. However, we do know from empirical studies that more socially isolated people are more likely to experience other negative aspects to their lives such as having the involvement of child protective services or experiencing physical and mental ill-health. Therefore, identifying gaps in personal and material resources and attempting to alleviate these may have important effects on other aspects of a person's life. The theory also has the advantage of paying attention to individual problems and wider difficulties caused by social and material inequalities, thus side-stepping the individual–environmental divide in social work.

Case management

So far this chapter has concentrated on different ways of directly providing practical help or therapeutic intervention to individuals and families. But much of what a social worker in contemporary society does involves something more akin to being a manager or broker. Case management, according to standards set in 2013 by the National Association of Social Workers in the US, is 'A process to plan, seek, advocate for, and monitor services from different social services or health care organizations and staff on behalf of a client.'

Case management may incorporate the activities already discussed—providing or arranging material or social help and promoting change—but while these specific tasks may be provided by social work and other agencies who specialize in particular areas (such as cognitive-behavioural therapy or crisis accommodation), the social worker as case manager will be responsible for overall planning, coordination, and reviewing service provision (see Figure 7). At its best, case management will lead

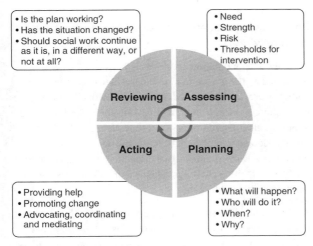

- Is the plan working?
- Has the situation changed?
- Should social work continue as it is, in a different way, or not at all?

- Need
- Strength
- Risk
- Thresholds for intervention

Reviewing   **Assessing**

Acting   **Planning**

- Providing help
- Promoting change
- Advocating, coordinating and mediating

- What will happen?
- Who will do it?
- When?
- Why?

7. **Case management process.**

to individuals and families receiving the individualized package of help that they need, for as long as they need it, without having to navigate many different agencies and thresholds. At their worst, case management systems can lead to social workers having to spend much more time completing administrative tasks than engaging directly with individuals who need help. They can block access to help due to overly high thresholds of need or risk having to be crossed before services can be provided. They may work against person-centred approaches by setting fixed timescales and mandatory procedures for everyone. However, a positive example is presented in Box 9.

In almost all cases, the provision of social work to individuals and families will take place after an assessment of need or risk. This assessment may be informal, perhaps not even written down, but increasingly in many countries assessments are formal, structured, and mandated by an employer or by the regional or national government.

Box 9 Case management to provide a 'team around the family'

In Wales, a family support service called Families First is mandated by the government to be provided in all local authority areas. It is expected that families with additional needs that require services from more than one agency will be offered a service called Team Around the Family. Needs and difficulties might include parental mental illness, substance misuse, domestic violence, or intellectual disabilities. Children may be disabled, exhibiting challenging behaviour, or not receiving good-enough parental care.

Previously, families with multiple needs have often been subject to many assessments by different agencies—there may have been considerable overlap of services being offered, and different professionals may not have shared knowledge and concerns. This is exhausting and confusing for the family and a waste of resources, and potentially important information might be lost. With a Team Around the Family one worker agrees to take the lead in ensuring that all agencies involved and the family plan together what help is needed and how it will be provided. This is (if it works well) an example of case management acting as an enabler rather than a bureaucratic barrier.

Assessment has become an important, formal stage in most fields of social work. There are usually guidelines, forms, or tools that are standardized on a local or national level. These may range from brief screening tools (e.g. 'does this person qualify for a service?', 'is this person at immediate risk of harm?') to a much more in-depth assessment that may be completed over several weeks or months. The practitioner will be guided on the areas to ask questions about, who to involve, and how to report the findings. This model relies on the professional or clinical judgement of the social worker to reach a conclusion. The areas to be covered are likely to be based on a consensus model—what is generally agreed by experts in the field to be 'best practice', although it may also be influenced by research evidence. The method of gathering data within an assessment framework may be varied and include observations and examining records, but it is likely to rely heavily on interviewing the service user and important people connected to them. This model has been criticized for being subject to personal bias.

In contrast is an actuarial model, which is usually based on comparing an individual's risk factors with risk factors known from research evidence to be statistically associated with a relevant outcome (such as child injury, death, or reoffending rates). Here the data recorded are largely numerical and the assessment conclusion will rely on whether the final score indicates a particular level of risk or need. While few, if any, social work services rely on actuarial-based assessments alone, they are used with increasing frequency to determine whether cases should be diverted to child protection interventions, or to calculate the risk of reoffending in criminal justice settings. Actuarial models reduce (but do not eliminate) the risks of individual bias, but have been criticized for leading to too many false positives or negative results due to the bluntness of the tools in comparison to the infinite variety of the human experience.

Assessment tools that use a combination of guided professional judgement along with some standardized, validated quantitative measures and that are carried out as collaboratively as possible with the family themselves and other professionals who know them are, we would argue, likely to provide the most comprehensive picture of risk, needs, and strengths of an individual or family. Analysis of the assessment data should lead to a care plan which lays out what is to be done, by whom, within what timescale, and with what objectives. A plan structured in this way means that when it comes to review the plan, which is a process formally mandated in most case management structures, it will be possible to examine the distance travelled since the plan was implemented and which aspects need to be adjusted.

Most people's circumstances change over time, and the lives of people who require social work services may be more unstable than others, perhaps due to violent relationships, insecure housing, or insecure incomes. Assessments and plans are never fixed and finalized, but need to be revisited regularly and sometimes on an emergency basis. For Adam, the fifteen-year-old who wishes to return to his previously violent father (Box 6), the social worker has been forced to revisit an earlier assessment that staying at home was too dangerous, in the light of Adam's expressed wishes, the lack of stable positive alternatives, and any changes made by his father in the intervening years.

From client-centred to citizen-directed social work

The voice of the person who is receiving social work services has been amplified and muted at various times over the decades, depending on the practitioner's ideological and methodological stance. Over the years, influenced by psychologists Carl Rogers and Abraham Maslow in the mid-20th century, many practitioners have claimed to take a 'client-centred' approach. In more recent years this has developed into more inclusion of clients in decision-making meetings and sometimes controlling their own budgets. In our own country, Wales, social services are now described as 'citizen-directed', and services are expected to be 'co-produced' by all interested parties. Although this is rhetorically powerful, squeezed budgets and increased demands for social work services can mean that citizens may have very limited resources to choose from in their citizen-directed support.

Since John E. Mayer and Noel Timms's study *The Client Speaks* (see Box 10), repeated studies with different groups (such as children, disabled adults, parents, older adults) and in different nations have found that individuals and families are looking for some core

Box 10 'The client speaks': listening to the experiences of service recipients

Over the years, service providers and researchers have begun to involve individuals more in providing feedback, and we can see some consistent and persistent strands in what service users say. In 1970 an early study of sixty-one clients' views was published in the UK by Mayer and Timms, called *The Client Speaks*. Perhaps surprisingly, this was one of the first studies to ask recipients of services what they thought about social work and social workers.

They found that many users of a social work service got quite different help than they wanted. In general they wanted help with poverty and help coping with someone else (e.g. a husband or child). They were often offered help with their personal insight through talking therapies. Some were baffled by the social worker and did not understand what was being offered. The most satisfied clients were offered practical help in addition to counselling and therapy—a psychosocial approach.

The Client Speaks was published at a time when a distrust of traditional open-ended casework was growing. As has been seen in this chapter, more task-oriented measurable approaches became popular, and the rise of case management has discouraged open-ended therapeutic relationships—at least in the public sector.

traits in the people who provide the help they receive. They want their social worker to be reliable, to be warm and approachable, to understand people in their situation, to listen, to be able to provide practical help, to be knowledgeable, and, often, to have a sense of humour. In some studies, these aspects have proven equally important to the service user as whether their lives improved as a result of the intervention. We return to how effective social work practice is in Chapter 6, but before that we broaden our scope beyond work with individuals to work with groups in Chapter 4 and communities in Chapter 5.

Chapter 4
Social work with groups

This chapter moves on from discussing social work with individuals and families to examine social work with groups. This is where usually unrelated people are brought together to receive some form of social work help or intervention in a group, or care is provided to groups of people in residential or day care. These are different approaches. Group work is a *method* of intervention, while group care may be undertaken for reasons of economy or efficiency. This chapter begins by discussing group work in the social work field. The second half of the chapter is about group care, mainly in residential settings.

What is group work?

Group work is more than just working with more than one person at once. There is a huge range in group work types and methods, as seen in Box 11, but all bring people together to fulfil some kind of purpose. Group work structures vary. Some are very informal and loosely structured groups, such as mutual support groups. At the other end of the spectrum some groups are highly structured and participants follow a pre-specified programme which is written up in a manual. Similarly, the style of group leadership will range from a directive leader to an enabler who prompts and facilitates discussion rather than directs it. Mutual self-help

Box 11 Some examples of group work in social work settings

Promoting individual change through group work methods

- Anger management groups with offenders
- Parenting programmes
- In-patient groups for people with mental illness
- Skills training for children in foster care
- Encounter groups or T-groups* to promote self-understanding, sensitivity to others, and training in group processes

* T = training

Mutual aid for those with shared experience

- Support groups for survivors of abuse
- Support groups for bereaved parents
- Support groups for kinship carers, foster carers, and adopters
- Alcoholics Anonymous

Groups whose primary aim is to promote change and further social justice

- Self-advocacy groups for people with learning disabilities
- Care leavers' councils or forums
- Community groups combating challenges in their community such as lack of facilities or gang violence

groups may have no formal leader at all, although group work theory would suggest that in such circumstances leaders will emerge through group processes.

All group work activities are likely to be promoted with the expectation that the members will gain something from being with each other, rather than learning or receiving help alone. The relationship between group members is usually at least as important as that with the group leader or facilitator. Learning will take place through these intergroup relationships, in addition to (or sometimes instead of) any formal transmission of new information. This attention to the relational aspect is what distinguishes group work from other situations such as a classroom, committee, or club. Groups may be open with members free to join or leave at any time, or closed with new members not permitted once the programme has begun. They also vary in size, although in classic group work theory six to twelve members is ideal.

Group aims usually relate to one or more of the following:

1. Using group work as a method of intervention to promote individual behavioural, cognitive, or attitudinal change;

2. Improving mood, self-esteem, and knowledge through meeting with others facing similar social circumstances in support groups;

3. Achieving change in an organization, community, or wider society through planning and taking action as a group;

4. Achieving enhanced self-awareness and sensitivity to others through participating in an unstructured group with built-in time for psychodynamic analysis.

How group work theories and methods developed

Group work began to be established as a method with a recognized theoretical base in the US in the 1920s and 1930s. It was taken up a little later in the rest of the Global North. There was considerable cross-fertilization between the fields of community organizing, adult education, and social work, but distinct use of group work in social work was established by this time. By 1934 it had 'section' status in the National Conference of Social Work, meaning that a stream of papers was presented under that heading. Techniques and processes were starting to be written down—to the extent that one speaker cautioned against overproceduralization.

Kurt Lewin, an American psychologist of German origin, pioneered early group work theories in the 1940s. He is credited with coining the term 'group dynamics', and for noting that the group itself forms a system that has an impact on its individual members. Lewin developed the T-group (training group), which also became known as sensitivity training groups or encounter groups. These groups allow participants to develop an understanding of group processes and of their own role within the group. Observation, reflection, and theory development are important parts of the group process.

Therapists trained through T-groups often went on to lead groups that became known as encounter groups, and were popularized by the well-known psychologist Carl Rogers (see Figure 8). Such groups have continued in use, although their popularity peaked

8. **An encounter group facilitated by Carl Rogers (on the right with glasses).**

between the 1960s and 1980s. While some members report great strides in sensitivity to others and self-awareness, they also carry risks due to the encouragement of disclosure of personal information and emotions. Encounter groups achieved some notoriety in the late 1960s and 1970s when some workers led nude groups.

In the 1970s Bruce Tuckman and Mary Ann Jensen developed a schema of group stages after studying the processes of T-groups. They came up with the very well-known rhyming sequence of *forming*, *norming*, *storming*, *performing*, and *adjourning*. This is inevitably a simplification that cannot describe every group experience, yet these stages have been observed in many research studies and can be recognized by anyone who has taken part in or led a group. They can also be helpful. It is perfectly usual for a group to go through a 'storming' period while group members challenge the aims or workings of a group, jostle for informal roles, and enter into conflicts. Acknowledging this can be reassuring for group members and leaders, and can encourage all to persevere until the group achieves some equilibrium and begins to 'perform'.

This term equilibrium is a reference to systems theory. We saw in Chapter 3 that systems theory has been an important influence on social work with individuals, in terms of understanding the individual within an ecological framework. The theory has been widely applied in group work and, along with family therapy, group work was an important site for developing systems theory in the 20th century. The theory pays attention to the whole group, beyond the interpersonal relations, and to group processes over time. Concepts such as feedback loops, communication flow, and equilibrium are drawn from the natural and physical sciences and applied to social processes.

Feedback loops refer to interactions between people in the family or social system that serve to facilitate change. Negative feedback loops maintain the current position. Group leaders using systemic techniques (either consciously or unconsciously) will be engaged in a process of stimulating group processes. For example they may analyse how communication patterns maintain current group norms and, if necessary, facilitate change. Systems theory may be the underlying theoretical framework for groups with a wide range of therapeutic aims.

In the 1960s and 1970s identity-based consciousness-raising groups became popular; particularly women's groups, gay and lesbian groups, and other groups that felt marginalized or disempowered in Western societies. These groups aimed to help members understand the structures and actions that oppressed and marginalized them. This new understanding often led members to demand change. Such groups were not necessarily initiated or facilitated by social workers, but the methods and aims chimed comfortably with the radical social work movements of the day. Similar groups have been used in social work settings such as women's refuges and community development projects and continue to this day (see Box 12), although they are more often labelled as 'advocacy', 'action', or 'support' groups.

Since the 1990s, evidence-based group work programmes have increased in influence, based on a new optimism that group teaching techniques based on social learning theories can change people's behaviour, understanding, and outcomes. Social learning theory, which can also be used in individual work, suggests that human behaviour is learned by individuals through interaction with their environment. Behaviour can be shaped or maintained by positive or negative reinforcement. How we think about our behaviour and relationships also play a role—hence the use of cognitive techniques and the development of cognitive-behavioural therapy. Social learning theory-based group work has become widespread in parenting education, probation, prisons, and mental health services.

Although some of the impetus for establishing groups based on techniques that have also been used with individuals may be

Box 12 Example: the European Power to Change groups

Towards the end of the first decade of the 21st century, a group of domestic abuse activists from Hungary, Italy, Estonia, Portugal, and the UK carried out a project funded by the European Union on group work in domestic abuse settings.

They developed a guide to running groups for victims and survivors called Power to Change that was based on shared experiences across these nations. The guide, published in 2008, claimed that bringing women together in such a way addresses the *social* aspects of domestic abuse, leaving other aspects of services to work on other needs such as shelter and prosecuting and educating abusers.

Women are quoted in the guide as having found out the following after attending Power to Change groups:

- That other women have had similar experiences
- That there were people who would believe them
- That there were positive changes they could make in order to have a more hopeful future

The groups are overtly feminist in ideology, and aim to address the public and political aspects of domestic violence. Their roots in consciousness-raising groups during the 1970s are evident, and the method is still promoted by some practitioners, particularly for marginalized or oppressed groups.

cost-effectiveness—more people can receive therapy or training at one time—there is also a recognition that the group can help with reinforcing or testing learning (see Box 13). Members of groups for people with specific problems or conditions can learn that they are not the only people with the same difficulties and can act as co-therapists by encouraging, reinforcing, or challenging each other.

Box 13 Example: Fostering Healthy Futures

This is a group work and mentoring programme for children aged nine to eleven in out-of-home care developed in Colorado, US. It lasts for nine months, and involves skills groups lasting thirty weeks for one-and-a-half hours per week. The skills development involves cognitive-behavioural activities including emotion recognition, problem solving, and anger management. Each child is also mentored by a graduate student in social work or psychology, who helps them to apply skills learned in the group to the real world. The ultimate aim is to reduce mental health and similar problems. Fostering Healthy Futures has been evaluated using a randomized controlled trial (see Chapter 6), and shows significant benefits for the children who take part.

Ethical issues in group work

There are a number of ethical issues that may be encountered and that require skill and knowledge on the part of the group leader. Many groups will involve members sharing personal information, and this may include disclosing experiences of abuse, sexual behaviours, criminal behaviours, and health information. Most groups will have established 'ground rules' at the start of the group or when new members join, and this is likely to include a rule of non-disclosure of information from within the group to others outside the group. The group leader, however, has no control over behaviour outside of the group and has to rely on members sticking to this agreement.

Another common 'ground rule' is non-violence, including verbal aggression. This may be a particularly important rule for those who attend a group designed to tackle anger, violence, or conduct disorders. While, at their best, groups will provide positive mutual reinforcement of pro-social behaviour, there is a risk that groups may reinforce or teach negative behaviours. Individual members may be bullied or scapegoated by other group members. Racist, sexist, homophobic, or other oppressive behaviours may be displayed and reinforced through group dynamics. Group members, such as sex offenders and drug users, could also make new negative relationships that they continue outside of the group. Skilled leadership, clear boundaries, and careful selection of group members can combat these risks.

Group care: groups in residential and day settings

The term 'group care' is used to indicate settings that people live in as well as settings that people attend in the daytime only. There are some shared features of residential care and day care. Mostly these involve more intense and sustained relationships than other models of social work.

First, the workers and people who receive the service will spend much more time together than in the casework model, where the social worker is office-based. Although many of the processes described in Chapter 3 will still take place in many group care settings—assessment, planning, reviewing, and purposeful and targeted interventions—there is inevitably also more emphasis on everyday interactions. Mealtimes, outings, sharing household tasks, and pursuing hobbies can be taken as opportunities for learning and sharing. More negatively, the intensity of this relationship means that even if the service user is perceived as challenging to care for, the worker must spend many hours with them with little relief. Likewise, the resident or person using the day service may have to tolerate spending time with a worker they dislike or whose style they find unhelpful.

Second, workers spend more time together and work in front of each other more than in office-based work. Relationships with each other are therefore more intense than in casework settings and their care work is more public. This provides opportunities for modelling positive relationships to those being cared for, mentoring and learning between staff members, support, and the ability to draw on different team members' strengths for different tasks. In a well-functioning team, a positive culture can emerge where respectful and therapeutic relationships within the setting can become the group norm for the entire home or centre.

Of course the opposite can also occur. As has been seen in scandals uncovered in many countries, negative worker cultures can develop where powerful figures impose a culture of indifference to the needs of those being cared for. This leads to poor standards, neglect, and sometimes abuse. Those being cared for may find it difficult or impossible to complain because they lack the means to do so, due to young or old age, disability, or a prevailing culture of disbelief.

Residential care

Residential care services have seen important shifts over the last century. There are a number of reasons why large-scale institutions have gradually become replaced, in many nations, with care based at home or in small, supportive group homes. One of these has been economics—in many circumstances it is generally cheaper to provide care for old and disabled people in their own homes than in hospitals or care homes. Also influential though, has been a human rights impetus. There has been a recognition that large-scale residential centres tend to develop institutionalized practices that do not respond well to individual needs and preferences. Children's and adults' rights to a family life have increased the use of foster care, small group homes, and care at home. Scandals about deliberate abuse and wilful neglect in residential care have also increased the stigmatization of residential care. Residential care, while remaining clearly part of the field of social work (often in combination with health care, psychiatry, education, and criminal justice) has become increasingly specialized in developed nations and reserved for people with the most complex care needs.

The role of residential care for children and young people in much of the Global North has shifted gradually from large residential homes, hospitals, and asylums which predominated until the 1950s, to family-based care. The shift for disabled children was slower. Butler and Drakeford, writing about British social work in the 1970s, draw on a 1973 issue of the British magazine *Social Work Today* to describe practices in that era. The magazine reported that there were 8,500 disabled children living in long-stay hospital wards, one-third of whom were never visited. Their basic need for physical care was met, but they were understimulated and had no toys. They were 'put to bed at 4pm on a summer evening so that nursing staff could get ahead with their routine work'.

Residential settings for children may be known as children's homes, group homes, or orphanages and are usually provided for those who have no parents or kin able or willing to care for them. In countries where extreme poverty and possibly armed conflict are present and health care is minimal, many children may be orphans. Children living in residential care in developing nations are likely to include babies and young children. In the Global North, in contrast, younger children are more likely to need care because of neglect, abuse, or because their parents cannot cope, and foster care with unrelated families or with kin has been the preferred model of care for children for several decades.

In the UK and the US, adoption, representing a complete legal transfer of parenting rights to new parents, tends to be seen as a desirable option for young children who cannot safely live with parents or kin. In most of the rest of the world this is an unusual step. Across Europe, patterns of use of residential care vary and it is used more widely in some nations than others. For example, positive results for children in residential care have been achieved in countries like Denmark and Germany using a model of social

Box 14 A typology of residential care settings

Secure settings—residents are required to live in the care setting by legal order. They may present a risk to themselves through self-harm, or to others through violent acts. Commonly, residents of secure settings have a diagnosed mental illness or personality disorder. The home or hospital ward is locked. Care may range from basic and essentially punitive to therapeutic.

Long-term residential care, traditional models—in traditional models of residential care, such as care homes for older people, disabled adults, and children, care is provided on a group basis for reasons of efficiency and economy. The home would aim to meet individual care needs with minimal attention to any therapeutic elements of the group.

Therapeutic communities—as described in more detail later in this chapter, such residential communities use the group aspects of living together as a therapeutic tool. The eventual aim is often to enable residents to live 'normally' in the community after recovering from mental illness or addiction.

Small group homes—as part of the move away from institutional care in many nations, disabled adults have been enabled to live in family-sized homes, with, for example, four residents and two or three support workers on a rota basis. These may be available as permanent homes or as preparation for independent living. In the case of preparation for independence, these may be available for young people leaving children's homes or foster care.

Rehabilitation or resettlement—some residential care homes are explicitly geared towards enabling people to move from institutional care (such as hospitals, prisons, and substance misuse treatment centres) and return to the community. They are sometimes referred to as 'half-way' houses.

Respite care—these offer part-time care to provide temporary breaks for the carer and those cared for.

pedagogy. Social pedagogues are graduates who have received a training akin to social work, but more directed at developing the individual and promoting change though the use of relationships and purposeful activities. In other Western nations, residential care for children is increasingly reserved for older children who find it very difficult to live in family settings due to trauma or behavioural problems, or who are compelled to live in secure settings because they have committed a serious crime or are thought to represent a danger to themselves or others.

Some children, particularly those with learning or physical disabilities, may live in residential or foster care on a part-time basis. This is known as respite care. It is designed to give the children's carers a break and also to enrich the child's experiences. Adults may also use respite care, again to provide carers with a break. Adults living alone may also need some respite care to recuperate after an illness or for regular rests when coping alone with a long-term condition.

Adults with learning disabilities, mental illness, and physical disabilities often live in small, supported group settings in the community and, as with children, there has been a shift away from large-scale residential facilities (see Box 14). This general trend across the Global North is part of what is often referred to as 'community care'—providing support for people in their homes and community facilities rather than in hospitals and residential homes.

Problems with residential care

In England, Wales, and Ireland, the legacy of the workhouse remained strong in the minds of the public throughout the 20th century. The 1834 Poor Law Amendment Act wiped out most 'outdoor relief'—the provision of basic help to the most needy in their own homes by their local parish. The need to ask for help was to be strongly disincentivized by requiring almost all those who had no other means of living to enter workhouses. Here conditions were harsh, with families separated by generation and gender, put to work, and provided with basic, often very poor, living conditions. A fear of entering the workhouse persisted long after their abolition.

In Scotland, 'poor houses' were used to a lesser extent than the rest of the British Isles, with outdoor relief remaining in place. Nonetheless, the poor houses that existed were not dissimilar to those south of the border. A workhouse historian Peter Higginbotham reports that a poor house in Edinburgh at the end of the 19th century had separate sections for 'Very Decent', 'Decent', 'Bastardy', and 'Depraved'. Similarly, in other nations folk memories remained of institutions of last resort for the destitute, such as poor houses and poor farms in America and workhouses in Belgium and the Netherlands. Such cultural memories mean that going into 'a home' is still regarded as an option of last resort in most cultures.

One consequence of residential care being reserved primarily for adults and children with the most complex difficulties is that residential settings can become challenging environments to work in. Despite this, staff are often poorly trained and low paid, exacerbating problems of staff quality and retention. This is of course a generalization, and there are examples of highly skilled and committed staff in residential care, but the complex needs of residents, coupled with the history of critical writings and scandals, have increased the marginalization of residential care in many nations. A number of influential writers and researchers in the middle decades of the 20th century critiqued the impact of institutionalization on individuals living in residential care. Two of the most influential were John Bowlby on infants and Erving Goffman on psychiatric hospitals.

Bowlby, whose ideas on attachment were introduced in Chapter 3, observed the impact of 'maternal deprivation' on babies and young children in alternative care settings during World War II in England, and published influential work on the importance of attachment to a primary carer. This work was influential in reducing the popularity of residential care for children. Ironically, many children living in family foster care are regularly moved from carer to carer, negating the opportunity to build attachments to a primary carer, while some young people in residential care form close bonds to staff members. Another irony is that in some countries boarding school, which may contain many institutionalized practices, is generally socially acceptable, with politicians from time to time suggesting that children in out-of-home care are sent to boarding school.

Goffman, an eminent sociologist, published his book *Asylums: Essays on the Social Situations of Mental Patients and Other Inmates* in 1961, based on his observations of a large state-run psychiatric hospital in the United States. Goffman described how the identity of the mentally ill person is formed and maintained as 'patient' or 'inmate' by institutional practices such as admissions procedures and case records, and how the individual can be dehumanized by these processes. Goffman reinforces his criticism of hospital practices by constantly comparing them to other 'total institutions' such as boarding schools, monasteries, the army and navy, prisons, and concentration camps.

These prominent criticisms of institutional care have been reinforced by a series of scandals uncovered about abuse and neglect in residential care settings (see Box 15). These include both ongoing, contemporary examples and historic abuse that has come to light decades later.

Advantages of residential care

Despite the scandals in residential care homes, which have greatly increased their stigma and unpopularity for all except for frail older people in much of the Global North, there are many examples where group living is promoted as a positive alternative to other care options. This is often related to settings which operate through

Box 15 Examples of scandals involving residential care

The Ely Hospital scandal 1967–9 highlighted the poor quality of care in some large institutions. Ely Hospital was a former workhouse in Cardiff that provided long-stay hospital care for people with learning disabilities. Some had lived there since before World War I. A care assistant reported the mistreatment of patients and staff corruption and there was a public outcry. A government-appointed committee of inquiry backed up the concerns. This scandal accelerated the closure of large-scale institutions for disabled people and also led to a formal system of inspections. Sadly, from time to time in modern care homes similar scandals are still exposed by care staff who act as 'whistle-blowers'.

In the early 1990s, after the break-up of the Soviet Union and the fall of the Berlin Wall, a spotlight was put on outdated institutional care practices in several countries. In particular, Romanian orphanages were highlighted as examples of very poor practice under the regime of former president Ceauşescu. Numerous television documentaries showing that children's basic needs were neglected led to a flood of Western concern, donations, and volunteers. Romania was required to show significant improvements before being admitted to membership of the European Union.

The Magdalene laundries or asylums were a series of institutions run by nuns, most notoriously in Ireland but also in England, Australia, and the US. The last one in Ireland was closed in 1996. Women who had transgressed moral codes were sent to them and often kept there against their will. There are many claims of systematic abuse from survivors, and the Irish Taoiseach (President) gave a full state apology to former residents in 2013.

a particular philosophy or method. Two examples of these are the Camphill Communities and the 'therapeutic communities'.

The first Camphill Community was founded in Aberdeen in Scotland in 1939 by an Austrian refugee, Dr Karl König, and a group of fellow Austrian refugees. They were inspired by the Austrian philosopher Rudolf Steiner to provide care for severely disabled children that was radically different from the standards of the day. At that time disabled children who were unable to attend mainstream education were usually either kept at home or in hospital wards. König's group attempted to let each child reach their full potential. Camphill communities developed to provide residential communities for adults with intellectual disabilities or mental health problems, usually in rural areas, with co-worker volunteers living and working alongside those with disabilities. Communities are now established in around twenty countries worldwide including Botswana, India, Estonia, Canada, and the US. Their underlying principles are respect, cooperation, equality, and the expectation that everyone can make a contribution. These principles have continued to challenge an emphasis on what disabled people cannot do—a deficit model—which places people with additional needs as passive recipients of care.

Therapeutic communities developed from several different movements and settings from the 1940s to 1970s in Britain and the US. These included a therapeutic group environment with soldiers in hospital in World War II, where the soldiers could get involved in mutual care and support, and the developing 'anti-psychiatry movement', which challenged the power relations and the perceived overmedicalization of mental illness in traditional psychiatric care. There are now therapeutic communities throughout the world, including in settings such as prisons and secure hospitals. Even in secure settings, therapeutic communities are usually entered on a voluntary basis as an alternative to mainstream prison or hospital care. Therapeutic communities are particularly used to treat long-standing problems that have proved intractable to many conventional treatments. These include personality disorders, substance misuse, and sex offending.

There are some definitional problems with therapeutic communities, insofar as the term has been used very broadly for group living environments that more or less adhere to principles of using the group as the main therapeutic tool. Beyond this there are different styles and ideologies. For example, some therapeutic communities will emphasize goals of personal growth, self-awareness, attachment, and relationships while others will place more emphasis on social aspects of change. There is a strong movement of therapeutic communities that promote democratic, non-hierarchical modes of living, while the equally strong 'concept-house' model is deliberately hierarchical and structured, allowing those attempting to recover from alcohol and drug addiction to move through stages towards addiction-free living in society. Therapeutic communities are now sometimes offered as a day service, with community members living at home but attending therapeutic sessions at least once a week.

Day care

Another form of group care is in day centres for those who require extra care. This might be provided for pre-school children, children and youths not attending school, and adults of all ages with extra needs such as physical and learning disabilities, neurological conditions, mental illness, dementia, and terminal illness. The care is provided for people who are able to remain in their own homes in the community but require therapy, social interaction, or physical care such as a hot meal and bathing.

Some would argue that a better term for day care is 'day services'. Thus the emphasis is changed from the person attending the day setting as a passive recipient of care, to a person who is utilizing services to meet their needs. This might arguably fit with a social model of disability, as discussed in Chapter 2. Others would argue that to disregard the word 'care' dehumanizes the provision of social welfare. Proponents of an ethic of care suggest that we should embrace the concept of care, recognizing that we are all interdependent in human society, that those who receive care may also give care, and that we all need care at times in our lives.

In many cases, day services will be formal resources that require referrals, assessments, and payments, often facilitated by a caseworker. There are, however, examples of community day care services that are open access. One example of a more open access model is Kids Company in London and Bristol. This is a charity that provides a wide range of services for vulnerable children and young people. It offers social work support, therapy, education, health services, and practical support, and young people can attend as much as they feel the need to for six days a week. These are similar to drop-in services provided to children living on the streets in some parts of the Global South.

Day care is commonly offered to older people with dementia whose carers, who may themselves be in frail health, need rest. The people living with dementia can receive specialist care and support such as memory groups, choirs, and physical care, and this type of service may allow them to continue living with their family and to avoid or delay residential care.

In this chapter we have discussed group work and residential care, but there is a great deal of overlap between these because some of the most innovative and important group work takes place *within* residential and day care settings—from memory groups in day services for people with dementia to therapeutic communities within prisons. Similarly, there is overlap with individual casework. Social workers working as caseworkers with individuals and families will spend much of their time arranging for their clients to attend therapeutic groups and to enter or leave residential and foster care. Group work also usually plays an important role in community social work, and we turn to this in Chapter 5.

Chapter 5
Community social work

As we noted in Chapter 1, the international definition of social work puts 'social change and development, social cohesion, and the empowerment and liberation of people' at the centre. This is despite the casework model described in Chapter 3 being dominant in the Global North. It will be seen in this chapter that social work in communities has played an important role throughout the history of social work and is still relevant and widespread today (see Box 16). It is central to the delivery of social welfare in the Global South.

In Chapter 2 we referred to the debate about where social work should best expend its energy as a profession—in addressing societal inequalities and improving distribution of resources, or in helping individuals in need of support and protection. This chapter explains how social work addresses the former aspect and attempts to work nearer the 'macro' rather than 'micro' level of human society.

What is community social work?

Community social work is concerned with improving the social and environmental context of the individual and family. At the level of the individual, it might involve analysing the impact of social networks and local environments on the person. This avoids

Box 16 Community social work examples

- A non-government agency in southern Africa is concerned that the social and physical needs of children orphaned by AIDS are not being met in rural areas. Social work educators train hundreds of 'para-social workers' who are paid to assess the needs of children in their local area and to make arrangements to ensure that their basic needs are met.

- A team of social workers working with adults with physical disabilities in a rural area of Europe notice that there is an increase in referrals concerning substance misuse among disabled adults in their community. They meet with the local disabled people's alliance, health workers, police, and youth workers to share concerns and plan some preventative programmes.

- An Israeli social worker develops an exchange programme for Arab and Jewish young people to promote cross-cultural understanding and reconciliation.

- An American not-for-profit agency working with inner-city children notes that the majority of their parents have experienced trauma through witnessing or being bereaved by gun crime. They develop group and individual counselling services.

the assumption that problems and solutions lie with the individual alone. Community social work might involve the development of new resources for a community. This could include physical resources such as new centres and social resources, such as support groups. Assessing need for these and putting them into place can be done in a variety of ways, with some contrast between community programmes that are planned and implemented on a 'top-down' basis and those that take a 'bottom-up' community development approach.

A top-down planning model recognizes that providers of services might be working in relative isolation from each other. To remedy this, senior managers in social work join together with those from education, health, housing, police, and so on to plan a coordinated response to groups in need of care in their area. This may involve the users of these services or their carers in making these plans, but this is not always part of the model. Community planning means that the needs of the local community are assessed and planned for.

Another top-down approach would be to implement a community resource to act as a preventative measure against the need for later individual help. This might be an area-based early intervention programme for young children, such as the Sure Start and Flying Start programmes in the UK. A needle exchange scheme to prevent blood borne viruses in injecting drug users and a carers' drop-in support centre are more targeted examples of preventative, community-based services.

Community development takes a bottom-up approach and aims to create social change. It helps communities to reach goals that are set within the community. That might be a new facility such as a school, clinic, play area, or affordable food store or a change in attitudes, opportunities, or behaviours such as reducing conflict or engaging people in new activities.

Community social work that is based on a community development model usually adopts a strengths-based approach. There is a belief that people can be enabled to reach their full potential and empowered to achieve things on their own rather than have solutions provided for them. Solutions are thought to be stronger and more effective if they are developed from within rather than imposed from outside. This theory can also apply to individuals and group work, but with community social work the added dimension is a belief that many problems are shared. Solutions are collective, rather than trying to work with one individual or family at a time.

This is the most overtly political form of social work. Social workers are aiming for social justice. It may involve a critique of casework-based social work as pathologizing people who are living in poverty, or experiencing other forms of oppression such as intimate violence or racism (see Chapter 2).

Different forms of community

What is a community? Many people think of communities as being neighbourhoods within towns and cities or other geographically defined areas like villages. But communities might also be people who share an interest, status, or faith. For example, deaf communities are networks of people who may be spread over a large geographical area but share a language and culture and often reject any notion that their hearing impairment is a deficit. Some online communities may have members spread around the globe, but feel that they belong to a community of people who have shared experiences such as being transgendered. Members of the same religion are often referred to as a community, especially if they are in a minority, e.g. 'the Muslim community' in a European nation.

It can immediately be seen that defining communities can be simplistic and mask diversity. 'The Muslim community', for example, will include people of all ages, classes, ethnic backgrounds, and linguistic heritage, and will often encompass a range of different Islamic schools of thought, including the categories of Shia and Sunni and diverse traditions within each of these. A neighbourhood too will include people with a wide range of experiences, needs, and interests. Social inequalities based on class, gender, race, sexuality, and disability exist within communities as well as between communities. A community social worker will have to work with diverse and sometimes competing interests as well as helping 'the community' achieve 'their goals'.

The term 'community' has been used right across the political spectrum, usually signifying a social system that has positive shared traditions. From the political right, communities might be encouraged to take care of their own members when welfare services are retrenched. From the left, the community might be seen as having collective strengths to resist capitalism and its consequences, such as the marketization of welfare services.

A 'third way' derived from the philosophy of communitarianism became popular in the 1990s in the US and the UK, which emphasized that the community provided a bulwark against extreme individualism and a positive environment for family life. Social work provided within this tradition was expected to provide opportunities for social development among the marginalized through help in gaining employment, and a preventative approach that emphasized early intervention by optimizing the life chances of young children in the poorest neighbourhoods.

Rights to opportunities and services, however, were seen to have been overemphasized in previous welfare regimes, with little regard for the social responsibility that was seen to come with them. Social workers and others implementing social policies were expected to ensure that individuals took up the opportunities offered to them, rather than the previous model which was seen as having promoted dependency. Critics, such as the social work academic Bill Jordan, have suggested that communitarianism fails to recognize or challenge economic inequalities, and instead of promoting redistributive policies it expects individuals and communities to find and take up opportunities for self-improvement.

Historical examples

There are numerous historical examples of community organizing, even if we only go back as far as the 19th century (we could go much further). Much of this was indigenous self-help, such as the early cooperative movement, founded in Rochdale, England, in the 1840s which started with a desire to establish a shop selling uncontaminated food at a fair price to mill workers, but soon mushroomed into a host of other community activities and inspired cooperative organizations worldwide.

Some early socialist and anti-colonialist movements also worked on principles of community organizing, while religious groups' concerns about the destitution and moral degradation among the newly urbanized poor led to some community responses such as Sunday schools and adult education.

The roots of what we now recognize as community social work might most clearly be seen in the university settlement movement, which we introduced in Chapter 1. In the 1880s, students and staff from Oxford and Cambridge universities began to establish settlements in London's poorest districts, beginning with Toynbee Hall in Whitechapel, East London. These early settlements followed a paper presented in St John's College, Cambridge, in 1883 by Canon Barnett: 'Settlements of University Men in Great Cities'. Settlements followed in Glasgow and Edinburgh in Scotland, Cardiff in Wales, and several university cities in the north of England and Bristol. The movement spread rapidly to the United States where settlements were founded in New York, Boston, and Chicago in the 1880s to 1890s. By 1910 there were more than 400 settlements in the US.

Settlements were also founded in many other cities worldwide between the 1890s and 1930s, including Bombay (now Mumbai) in 1926. In 1899, the first full-time professional training course was opened. The Institute for Social Work Training in Amsterdam offered five fields of study over two years. This included 'Toynbee work', thus establishing community approaches at the heart of professional social work.

An article by one of the founders of the Cardiff University settlement, a professor of Greek, Ronald Burrows, in 1905 sums up the impetus of some of the settlement pioneers:

It is vitally important for the well-being of the nation that the words College and University, Academic and Cultural, should stand in the eyes of the masses not for aloofness and exclusiveness but for breadth and sympathy.

In Cardiff this meant students and staff engaging several times a week in organizing clubs, classes, outings, entertainments and holidays for men, women, and teenage boys and girls, many of whom were very low waged, in precarious work, or unemployed. Professor J. S. MacKenzie, who held a chair in logic and philosophy, moved with his wife from their comfortable suburban home to live in the working class district of Splott where the settlement was located.

There is much in these early movements that seems to our modern sensibilities to be patronizing and sexist—an emphasis on the domesticity of the women and girls, for example. However, the thrust of the work was a belief in mutuality. Lack of opportunity and education were seen as key barriers. This can be contrasted to the work of other charities of the same era that emphasized unwillingness to work and weak character as underpinning much of the suffering of the poor. Charities that rescued children from poor communities, or assessed families' needs individually, went about their work in different ways from those in the settlements that sought to raise the morale and morals of the whole neighbourhood. The experience of living and working in settlements understandably led to the enlightenment of the middle class volunteers, too. A faculty member called Miss Bull interviewed former settlement workers in the 1960s. She quotes a woman who as a student teacher spent an evening trying to run a girls' group in Cardiff but found the girls quite able to organize their own boisterous session and concluded that: 'We graduates left at the close of the evening much less conceited than we went in.'

Many important figures spent some of their youth in settlements, such as William Beveridge, who wrote the report that led to the founding of the welfare state in the UK after World War II, and Clement Atlee, the Labour prime minister who implemented the welfare state. Settlements were important in providing early examples of social work involvement in social change, social organizing, and analysing social problems within wider social structures. Early community surveys and research were conducted by settlements to understand how problems were caused and sustained beyond the level of the individual. Women involved in settlement work became active international peace campaigners in World War I. The National Association for the Advancement of Colored People (NAACP) in the United States arose out of settlement activities.

In Britain, as social work developed as a profession in the middle decades of the 20th century it became identified with individual casework. This changed with a brief flourishing of community work ideas in social work education and practice between the 1960s and 1980s. A report of a committee on training for community work, supported by the Calouste Gulbenkian Foundation, stated in 1968 that: 'It is already clear that there is a community work element in the day-to-day activities of a large number of staff hitherto thought of as caseworkers only' (p. 17).

The authors point to the increased recognition of the impact of social relationships, cultural and environmental factors on the individual, and an increased need to coordinate between services at local authority level. They found that community work was recognized as an expected role in many social work training programmes, but was less common in teaching and youth work programmes. In the same year, the influential government-commissioned *Seebohm Report* led to unified local authority social service departments in England and Wales, which were designed to be non-stigmatized, comprehensive sources of help for all those in need in a local area. Community work was part of this vision: 'The new department will... enable the greatest possible number of individuals to act reciprocally, giving and receiving service for the well-being of the community.' Local authorities in the 1970s responded by employing neighbourhood workers alongside their more traditional caseworkers.

Internationally, in the 1970s community work as a concept gained ground and was incorporated into many professional training courses, including social work. Nonetheless, this tended to provoke continuing debate about the place of political action in social work and the perceived tension between work with individuals and work at a community level. This is exemplified by a meeting in 1976 of a group of social work educators from nine European countries and Israel, who met in Edinburgh to debate the best ways to teach community work. This was an era in which radical social work was gaining ground. It was clear that there were tensions as to how overtly political community work should be, with discussion about the place in social work of organizing and taking part in peaceful demonstrations and other non-violent actions. Debates about the balance to be reached in social work education between community and casework approaches appeared to be widely shared across the ten nations.

Despite community work in the 1960 and 1970s being an important part of the work of social workers and the state organizations that employed them, the majority of community workers in the UK did not hold a social work qualification and instead were youth workers, housing workers, teachers, health workers, and those without formal qualifications. In 1982 the Barclay Committee report into the roles and tasks of social workers again promoted community social work in neighbourhoods as a positive way forward, but in that decade individualized approaches instead became yet more dominant in the profession. Community work became, in the main, something that took place at a distance from social workers' casework.

Similarly, in the 1960s there was much debate in the US about whether there was a place for professional social workers in community work, and what role social activism should play in social work activities. Nonetheless, community development as part of the 'macro' strand of social work education retained importance in the 1960s, 1970s, and 1980s, after which it waned in comparison to clinical specialisms. By the mid-1990s fewer than 5 per cent of social work graduates had majored in 'macro' practice, although some schools of social work retain this today as a clear option for student social workers to specialize in.

In the Global South, schools of social work became widespread in the mid-20th century. Although largely adopting European and North American models of the three strands of social work—casework, group work, and community work—it was the last that was seen as most relevant in developing nations. For example, in 1968 a meeting in Africa of the first International Conference of Ministers Responsible for Social Welfare recommended that a priority in social welfare training must be development work.

In the 1970s a movement of 'indigenization' of social work rejected the wholesale adoption of Western models of social work, favouring instead locally developed models. In Latin America these were more overtly political, aimed at organizing the poor, encouraging participation, and consciousness-raising. These practices were influenced by liberation theology in the South and Central American Catholic Church and by Paolo Friere, whose radical ideas about education transferred easily to social work. Friere's ideas began to influence radical social work in the Global North, in contrast to the previous transplantation of Eurocentric social work to Latin America. Sadly, some of these indigenous radical social work movements were severely repressed by military dictatorships such as Pinochet's regime in Chile.

Contemporary community social work

Community development is still a thriving practice globally, but the extent to which this is accepted as being a part of *social work* varies. On the whole, social work in the Global North is concentrated on individual or clinical therapeutic work, risk management, group work, and organizing and providing care. In the UK, community development is mainly located outside of the local government social services departments where most qualified social workers are employed, and instead it is usually carried out in the voluntary and non-profit sectors (see Box 17) or through government area development programmes.

Similarly, in the US, although community work is a recognized skill in social work, the providers are mainly from the not-for-profit sector, with the professional social work role placing more emphasis on individual help and protection. A workforce survey in 2008 by the National Association for Social Work found that only 2 per cent of social workers' time was spend in community organizing and policy development.

It is in the Global South, however, that community social work retains a central role. Reports about social work graduates from countries throughout the Global South suggest that they are

Box 17 Example: FARE—Family Action in Rogerfield and Easterhouse

FARE is a project in Glasgow, Scotland. It was founded by Bob Holman with local residents. In an echo of the university settlements, Holman was a university professor of social work who went to live and work with the residents of a city area where people face economic and social challenges. Over more than twenty years they have built a large thriving, multifaceted centre meeting the needs of residents of all ages, and addressing health, violence, isolation, and many other issues. Holman describes this work as community social work, and it provides a successful alternative social work model in a system dominated by individualized responses.

likely to find employment with non-government agencies working in the area of community development, and are more likely to be called development workers than social workers. In areas of widespread deprivation, where welfare, health, and education systems are under-resourced, community development approaches are likely to be more effective than individualized interventions.

It is not just for practical reasons, however, that community development approaches are central to the indigenization of social work. Individual approaches are perceived as being particularly Western. In many cultures the collective good of the family, clan, village, or wider community is regarded as more important than the fulfilment of individual aims. Social work must respond to this in its theory and methods of intervention, and many social work programmes in universities in Africa, Asia, and the Pacific region are attempting to develop more culturally relevant curricula.

The community development concept of local solutions that arise from the world view of local people means that imposing Western European and North American social work models as norms to the rest of the world will not always be successful. In 1997 the South African government published a White Paper on social welfare that epitomizes this critical response from the Global South (see Box 18).

The lesson that local, indigenous solutions are more sustainable than 'off-the-shelf' services and programmes imposed from outside is an important one. While there were undoubtedly preconceived ideas about what would be good for the residents of impoverished neighbourhoods among early pioneers of the settlement movement, many solutions began to evolve through sustained relationships with local residents and a deeper understanding of their needs.

Box 18 The South African government's White Paper on social welfare, 1997

The government had inherited an unequal social welfare regime from the Apartheid era. The White Paper aimed to create a more democratic and locally developed approach that would have equal access to resources at its core. Its front page uses the terms social justice, community development, and community participation, signalling an intention to develop a social welfare regime that was more collective than individual. The paper criticized existing social work services as being too rehabilitative rather than developmental in orientation.

The positioning of this approach as essentially African can be seen in the final item of a list of guiding principles—Ubuntu: people are people through other people, so the principle of caring for others' well-being and the spirit of mutual support will be fostered. This is a reminder that in the southern African region the term for being human is defined through people's interconnectedness.

Jonathan Dickens and Victor Groza, writing in the journal *International Social Work* in 2004, reflected on the response to the Romanian children's home scandal mentioned in Chapter 4. Appalled by the conditions of the homes, two large movements began which attempted to help. One was the 'rescuing' of over 10,000 children in one year through international adoption. The rush to do this meant that not all were carefully planned or even legal. The second movement was the influx of hundreds of aid agencies who provided supplies and volunteers. These were largely uncoordinated and paid little attention to the existing workers, few of whom were trained to provide better care before the majority of organizations left within a few years. Both of these movements were disempowering to Romanian workers and authorities and did not help produce sustainable change.

> **Box 19 Community social work: Integrated Village Development Project, Krishnagiri, India**
>
> This project, like most community development projects, started small and has gradually expanded in a sustainable fashion. Its scope includes sanitation, education, reliable clean water supplies, and micro-financing.
>
> The founder apparently first attempted a micro-financing scheme with the men of the village, but this was unsuccessful. When he switched to lending money to women for self-help schemes and encouraging savings the project was transformed and became self-sufficient. The organization reports that over a million women working in mutual groups of twelve to twenty members saved money and took out small loans between 1979 and 2014.

Notions of 'the community' risk masking social and economic divisions within communities, and one of the most profound divisions in many societies is the unequal status of men and women. Some of the strongest community development projects principally involve women, who are seen in some cultures as more likely than men to be committed to the well-being of their families and communities. In India, a former priest-turned-social worker, Kulandei Francis, founded the Integrated Village Development Project (IVDP) in Krishnagiri in 1979, which works primarily with women (see Box 19).

The future of community social work

In much of the Global North, professional state-provided social work has become centred on the individual and their family. The heyday of radical social work and attempts to promote social change through community organizing have faded since the 1970s. While community projects still thrive throughout the Western world, and their work could comfortably be defined as 'social work'—assessing local need, mobilizing local activity, providing practical help and advice, group work, etc.—their organizers and workers may not label themselves as social workers, but instead as youth and community workers, early years workers, community education workers, health care workers, and so on.

In the Global South, however, community social work has continued to play a central role in the work of social workers and others engaged in social welfare projects. Indigenous social work, which is rooted in the values, beliefs, and practices of local communities, has been increasingly identified as more effective and appropriate than models transferred directly from Western Europe and North America.

Contemporary world challenges demand an evolving social work response. Climate change is contributing to environmental disasters that have the greatest impact on the poorest and most vulnerable people. The National Association of Social Workers in the US maintains a database of trained disaster mental health professionals. The Hurricane Katrina disaster in New Orleans in 2005 saw many social workers getting involved in providing emergency social work assistance to displaced people and, later, helping to rebuild communities. In Europe, social workers may develop programmes to divert Muslim youth from potential radicalization and attempts to fight in conflicts overseas. Worldwide, social workers work with police to identify and protect children featuring in Internet pornography.

In southern Europe, social workers have responded to the extreme cuts in public services and family incomes in the financial crisis after 2010 by taking political action. This was despite a relatively conservative history of social work heavily influenced by the Church. In Spain, where public services were subject to severe cuts, social workers joined with clients of social services to create the Orange Tide movement. Supported by their national association, they were highly visible in street protests using music and dance to call for 'no cuts to social services'. In Greece, social workers refused to implement government policies which required them to approve the disconnection of electricity supplies to indebted families and to register the presence of immigrant children in nurseries.

In most of these situations social media can act as a threat, for example in encouraging the sexual exploitation of children and spreading oppressive ideas. On the other hand, the rapidly changing online world can also be used by social workers to build new communities. Online forums for adopters, for example, share information and support and make people who are geographical dispersed feel connected to a community of similar people. Physical or virtual protests against social policies, as in the Spanish example, can be organized quickly through social media, and in some cases have restored the radical social work ideas of the 1960s and 1970s of social worker as agitator and organizer.

Chapter 6
Does it work and how do we know?

Should social work be thought of as science or art? What kind of knowledge do social workers need? What should they be learning when they do their professional training? Should the outcomes of social work help be tested using experimental methods, and if so how much weight should we put on that testing compared with other kinds of evidence? And what do we know about effective helping? Do some approaches seem to work better than others? These are the questions addressed in this final chapter.

Science or art?

Social work is informed by the social sciences. That statement is true enough, but it does not tell us much about social work's academic underpinning, because the social sciences are subject to a wide range of theoretical and methodological influences from across the arts, humanities, and natural sciences. To draw out the tensions, as we have tried to do throughout this book, we describe here two contrasting visions of what kind of knowledge should inform social work.

The first vision is social work as art. Hugh England wrote a book with this title in the 1980s. Social work as art means a strong emphasis on the creative skill of the individual practitioner and the meanings of social interactions to all involved. Proponents of this view might observe that social work is an essentially moral activity, and that humane responses to the problems people face will inevitably have to be individualized. What helps keep one suicidal person alive, for example, may not work for another. The personality and style of the individual social worker is essential to the social work process, and unique relationships with clients are the basis of everything that follows. Social work, according to this vision, cannot be codified or proceduralized, because it is infinitely variable and practitioners need space to be creative with the unique situations they encounter on a daily basis.

The second vision is quite different—that of the scientific practitioner. This perspective would emphasize the application of generalizable knowledge from social science, and especially quantitative evidence. Even the social work as art perspective would draw on some quantitative evidence, for example statistics about the limited life chances of people in poverty. But a scientific perspective on social work would use evidence from experiments to guide practice. That is, practitioners with this point of view would try to use only those approaches which have been scientifically tested and found to be effective. Other approaches, however intuitively appealing, would be rejected. This approach is termed evidence-based practice.

Few real people actually take a position fully in line with either of these visions. Most are of course somewhere in between. However, social workers do need to decide where they stand on these debates, which tie in with ideas about epistemology (how do we know?) and ontology (what is real?). As has been noted throughout this book, social work knowledge is contested and there is not the same consensus about the core as we find in some other well-established professions such as medicine and law. It can be the case that even within the same country, considerable variation is found between social work curricula in different universities. Some, for example, emphasize more psychological approaches and some are more oriented towards sociology.

The content of social work education can be a controversial political issue. In November 2013, the UK's education minister at the time, Michael Gove, made a high-profile speech in which he described social work training as placing too little emphasis on individual agency and personal responsibility for behaviour change, instead promoting the idea that people are disempowered by social injustice. This in turn provoked a response from the Association of Professors of Social Work which defended the centrality of social justice to social work practice.

What counts as evidence?

Social work is a field without an extensive evidence base, when compared to the major social science disciplines and better-established applied fields such as education or health care. At this point we consider the evidence base, which is one important aspect of social work knowledge, along with theory and the practice wisdom derived from the lived experience of providing or receiving social work services.

The different visions of social work as science or art have different implications for research evidence. A scientific model means that a degree of certainty can be achieved about the real outcomes of social work if an experimental research design is used. According to this model, the 'gold standard' is the randomized controlled trial (RCT). The main point of an RCT is to compare people who have received an intervention with people with the same characteristics who have not. To only measure outcomes before and after social work services are used will not tell us about the effectiveness of those services, because we cannot know what else has happened to these clients that might have affected their outcome measures. If, however, we have a large enough group of people who are randomly allocated to one of two groups—intervention or control group—then it ought to be that the only systematic difference between the two groups is whether or not they had the social work help.

RCTs are, however, not universally accepted in social work research. It is often impossible to set one up, because of practical constraints and lack of awareness or acceptance of the RCT rationale on the ground in social work services. Some would dispute the validity of a hierarchy of knowledge with RCTs at the top. They might do this on the basis of a deep scepticism about the possibility of certainty in social science research, or about the possibility of really removing differences between intervention and control groups through randomization. They might also think that the kinds of measures typically used in RCTs are too crude, or that randomization of individuals to receive a service or not is unethical.

Some of these reservations are in turn challenged by proponents of more RCTs in social work. In particular, the ethics point is turned on its head by those who argue for evidence-based practice, who would say it is unethical to use social work help which has not been tested and found to be effective in achieving its stated outcomes, however acceptable the approach might be to people taking part.

There are quite different priorities for research evidence promoted by proponents of qualitative approaches. Qualitative research can provide insights into what social work processes and relationships mean to both worker and client. Only by observing interactions in offices, community centres, and clients' homes, by reading key social work documents, and by hearing people's views expressed in their own terms can we really find out what is going on in social work. Even if we have experimental evidence that an intervention seems to work in achieving its stated aims, we cannot know why it has worked unless we can observe the process and ask people how it went, processes which both require qualitative data. These data can come in a range of forms, including visual data such as drawings and videos; documentary data such as case files; field notes made by observers, who may also have themselves been participants; and social work talk from naturally occurring interactions or from reflective interviews with a researcher.

Either approach can and should include clients' own evaluations of social work, as seen in the landmark Mayer and Timms study in Chapter 3 (Box 10). However, the scientific approach would tend to be more sceptical about evidence that relies exclusively on client satisfaction, as it could be argued that social work which is popular with clients but does not achieve its other stated objectives, such as improvement in quality of life or reduction in offending, is not effective social work.

There are different research traditions in different countries. So within the English-speaking world there is a strong emphasis in the United States on quantitative evidence about social work and RCTs where possible. In the UK, Australia, and Canada there seems to be more of an interest in critical qualitative approaches. This was confirmed by recent surveys of social work doctorates in the UK and US, which found that primarily quantitative approaches dominated in the US and primarily qualitative ones in the UK.

Why is robust evidence of outcomes important?

Probably the strongest argument in favour of RCTs and other studies which use control groups, such as non-randomized ('quasi-experimental') comparisons, is that some evidence points to the potential for social work interventions to have harmful effects. Practitioners are invariably well-meaning when putting together social work programmes. Even though they may not be without vested interests in a certain approach—for example perceptions of its success may provide them with continued employment or allow their organization to expand—the vast majority of social workers firmly believe in the approaches they espouse. However, there are examples of when well-meaning interventions have been tested in experimental conditions and found to have the opposite effect to what was intended.

One likely explanation for the false positive finding that Scared Straight (see Box 20) was successful, according to the testimony of participants, is the general tendency for people to grow out of crime as they age. If a group of young offenders who have taken part in a social work programme are followed up over time, inevitably some will have stopped offending or reduced the frequency and seriousness of their offending. But a different story can emerge if they are compared with another group with very similar characteristics but who have not attended the programme. The negative results for Scared Straight might suggest that

---

Box 20 Why robust evidence of outcomes is important: the example of Scared Straight

Scared Straight (see Figure 9) was a social intervention which seemed to make sense. It involved getting ex-offenders who had done time to warn younger offenders of the error of their ways, using their own stories as the examples of how it can all go wrong. It was the subject of a high-profile documentary in the US in the late 1970s, which was popular enough to have spawned two follow-up programmes tracking the same offenders over time, and a spin-off television series.

In the television programmes, individuals have given testimony as to how Scared Straight helped them change direction and get out of crime. However, rigorous evaluation has turned the assumption that this approach must be helpful on its head. Meta-analysis by Anthony Petrosino and colleagues, of seven randomized controlled trials, found the intervention to be on average more harmful than doing nothing. This shows the importance of having a control group.

9. Documentary about Scared Straight. Image from cover of DVD.

contact with hardened old cons can have the opposite effect to that intended. It might somehow make a life of crime seem like a more attractive option, perhaps making it seem strangely glamorous, regardless of how grim are the tales of adversity.

An analogous situation would be the worrying finding that some universal school-based suicide prevention programmes have increased students' hopelessness and beliefs in the acceptability of suicide. Telling young people stories of woe will not necessarily have the desired effect. It might make suicide seem like a less extreme response to personal difficulties, or may even provide a model for them to frame their difficulties in suicidal terms.

Another famous example of social work damage is the Cambridge-Somerville pair-matched study of a youth offending prevention scheme from the 1930s. It involved intensive befriending from a 'counsellor' for boys in an industrial area of Massachusetts over a period of five years. The boys taking part in the trial were either considered as 'difficult' or 'average'. Apart from the counsellors' visits, other elements included help with family problems, educational support, medical and psychiatric consultation, and attendance at summer camps and youth organizations such as the Scouts. The approach was very much rooted in the psychodynamic thinking of the time, with the counsellor having a 're-parenting' role.

Joan McCord's thirty-year follow-up noted that despite the overwhelming majority of the men as adults speaking highly of their experience, and many saying it had helped them, in fact on many measures the control group, who had the same age, backgrounds, and level of risk for 'delinquency', fared better. Men in the intervention group were more likely to be convicted of at least a second crime, to have alcoholism, mental illness, heart disease, and stress-related illness, and to die young. They were also more likely to have lower-prestige occupations and less likely to report their work as satisfying.

These examples of apparently benign help having damaging effects speak of the importance of comparing social work service users with a very similar group of people who have not experienced the service. Nothing can provide evidence as strong as this, and there should therefore rightly be a hierarchy of evidence with RCTs at the top. The very best source of evidence for those deciding which practice approaches to use is a systematic review, which consists of a rigorous procedure for locating studies, sorting them into a hierarchy of evidence from RCTs down, and where possible combining comparable results into one single meta-analysis which allows for an overall conclusion to be made about effectiveness.

However, the need for robust research certainly extends to other kinds of studies, including those which rely exclusively on qualitative data. Rigorous evaluation of social work should include observation of front-line practice, in order to document how recommended interventions are actually carried out. There are many examples of ethnographic (i.e. observation-based) research uncovering problems of implementation. For example, ethnographic studies of child protection work in England and Wales in the 2000s by Sue White and colleagues documented the problems in practice, with social workers trying to conform to set timescales and work within unwieldy information technology systems.

RCTs should ideally include qualitative research alongside quantitative measures. In recent years, realist trials have been emerging where the realistic evaluation approach of Ray Pawson and Nick Tilley is used alongside the traditional RCT design. This means that as well as evidence of outcomes we can understand social work processes and which particular mechanisms are most helpful. It is worth noting again, however, that RCTs are often not feasible in social work. They are also quite costly and are therefore more difficult to enact in poorer countries. Most often in social work there is no experimental evidence available. It is important that in this context social workers reflect critically on what they are doing and measure the outcomes of their own practice. And even where strong evidence does exist to inform the choice of effective help, social work encounters will still require sophisticated individualized judgements. There can be no silver bullet in social work—no magic pill.

What do we know works?

Brian Sheldon and Geraldine Macdonald are social work academics who have been relatively isolated voices in the UK in arguing for evidence-based practice. Their excellent and very readable book *A Textbook of Social Work* provides a useful summary of some general trends from studies of the effectiveness of social work.

They note the importance of a logical fit between evidence on the nature of the problem to be addressed and evidence on the effectiveness of interventions. One example they give is the physical abuse of children. They describe four different sets of causal circumstances: (1) parents' experiences have left them ill-equipped in terms of skills to deal with difficult behaviour and they are liable to misattribute its intent; (2) substance use dulls parents' abilities to respond to children's needs; (3) parents' socialization has led them to be impulsive and they have not learned anger control; and (4) the family circumstances are so depressing that any difficult behaviour from children is seen to be the straw that breaks the camel's back. The important thing to note, according to Sheldon and Macdonald, is that each of these situations will require a quite different kind of help. Any one-size-fits-all approach is likely to be ineffective.

Their next generic observation is that most of the evidence of effective practice relates to specialist preventative work, which focuses on emerging problems before they become entrenched and difficult to turn around. Evidence suggests that rigorously evaluated interventions fare well. There is something about the attention paid to particular projects that are well thought out and carefully delivered with evaluators hovering which brings good results. Both categories of social work—prevention and evaluated programmes—tackle root causes rather than treating symptoms in individual cases.

There are many examples where effective interventions are delivered via group work. Sheldon and Macdonald note that two important features seem to be that (1) the problems of group members should be similar in character rather than people attending the group simply because they have some kind of problem, and (2) group content needs to include some new behavioural options. They note that groups which are introspectively focused on the dynamics within the group itself have not been found to be effective. As well as intervention content, the personal style of the worker is important and could be considered necessary though not sufficient for effective helping. They highlight three elements: non-possessive warmth, genuineness, and accurate empathy.

Edward Mullen and Joseph Shuluk have provided an overview of the major evidence reviews conducted on social work interventions since 1990. They reach the optimistic conclusion that roughly two-thirds of the clients of social workers gain some benefit from this help. This positive conclusion still holds after controlling for researcher bias and publication bias, although these do inflate positive findings. They reach their conclusions on the basis of these reviews of effectiveness studies (see Box 21).

Box 21 Examples of positive social work outcome evidence

Kinship care for abused or neglected children

It would obviously not be considered ethical to randomly allocate a group of children who have to be cared for outside their birth families to either go to foster homes or relatives. The best comparison available therefore is from quasi-experimental

Box 21 (Continued)

studies, where those with relatives (kinship care) are compared with those in mainstream foster care.

A systematic review published in 2014 by Marc Winokur and colleagues included 122 quasi-experimental studies, which featured 666,615 children. A meta-analysis was conducted, combining the results of seventy-one of the studies. This found that children in kinship care experienced better outcomes than children in foster care on several measures, including behaviour problems, psychiatric disorders, well-being, placement stability, and institutional abuse. The evidence is limited and subject to various biases.

The study designs cannot remove the possibility that the two groups being compared are different to begin with, and the children in foster care were already at higher risk of experiencing the negative outcomes before being placed in care. However, the limited evidence does offer support for the continued use of kinship care.

Case management for frail older people

Emily You and colleagues published a systematic review in 2012 of ten RCTs and five quasi-experimental studies on the holistic care of older people living in the community. Case management systems included assessment and the planning, coordination, and monitoring of care. The fifteen studies used a range of different outcomes.

The review found that case management improved psychological health and well-being compared with control groups in five out of seven studies which measured these outcomes. There was also evidence from three of the studies that unmet need was lower in the case management group. However, there were mixed results for physical and cognitive functioning and impact on carers, with no clear benefit from case management in these domains.

As academics with strong social work identities we welcome this good news of course, but there is a big problem with this conclusion, namely that the studies that underpin the reviews they have summarized tend to be focused on a specific intervention which uses a particular theoretical approach to help ease a specific problem. Much routine statutory social work practice is likely to be fairly generalist and perhaps more focused on bureaucratic processes than on using any particular theoretical model. The 'two-thirds' that Mullen and Shuluk refer to are two-thirds of people in effectiveness studies. We are very doubtful that these interventions are representative of the general pool of social work approaches used in practice.

Some of the reviews they considered evaluated theoretical differences. Mullen and Shuluk's overall conclusion is that theoretical differences do not account for differential outcomes. However, there is some evidence that for specific problems some kinds of interventions are more effective than others. For example, the 1997 review by Bill Reid and colleagues found better outcomes in many problem areas for behavioural and cognitive-behavioural methods, and interventions with multiple components were often more effective than those consisting of a single component. Sheldon and Macdonald, writing in 2009, similarly note that there is a raft of evidence for the effectiveness of cognitive-behavioural approaches for a range of issues:

> The results of systematic reviews and experiments show that in juvenile justice and probation, in cases of depression, in relapse prevention, in schizophrenia, in the field of child behavioural problems, in helping families to cope with an autistic child, and so forth, cognitive-behavioural approaches never come second to anything. (p. 64)

It can immediately be seen, however, that the problems listed here are all more or less focused on individual change. Much of the evaluation effort in social work research has been centred on behaviour change interventions. This is in part because in the affluent countries where research has financial support, behaviour change is a big part of what social workers do. As we noted earlier in the book, behaviour change should not be dismissed as simply social control—its benefits can be felt in the improved quality of life of individuals and even sometimes whole communities. However, much more evidence is needed about social work that is more oriented towards changes at a community level. Some such evidence exists in the public health field, but social work should aim to achieve an evidence base which is spread across its many facets.

Concluding thoughts

Social work may have a relatively small evidence base for its effectiveness compared to some other helping professions. And indeed it may not always work. It is, however, undoubtedly a humane response to the problems of modern living. As such it is almost certainly not going away. It is likely to change considerably in coming years, with the impact of increased migration, new technology, and more private service delivery. The rise in personalized and client-controlled support in some countries could mean fewer social workers will be needed, or at least there could be a major shift in emphasis towards client empowerment.

We end the book by turning to fiction. Although we are broadly sympathetic to a scientific model for informing effective social work, there is also a need to turn to the arts and humanities. Fiction, drama, and film can be very useful in social work education, for developing empathy and generating sophisticated reflection about the personal and moral dimensions of everyday social work practice.

We recommend György Konrád's powerful novel *The Case Worker*. Konrád was a children's welfare supervisor in Hungary in the 1960s, and he portrays the grim reality of the cases encountered in day-to-day practice, albeit of course in a piece of fiction, in which the caseworker is the main protagonist. At the end of the novel, which was first published in Hungarian in 1969, Konrád presents an extensive list of the kinds of people the caseworker will continue to meet as clients, on into the future. His tone and language are not the respectful ones we would expect today, and he certainly regards his clients and their profound social problems as 'other'. However, the multiple scenarios of emotional and material deprivation from his time are rather beautifully described. And after this long list, he ends on a note of common humanity and collectivity, with a simple statement of the value of togetherness.

It is impossible to imagine a world without social work, as long as social inequality persists. Someone needs to reach out and respond to social suffering, if help provided by family members and friends is not enough. What follows are just a few excerpts from the closing five pages of Konrád's novel:

> In the meantime I wait for my clients... Let all the children come, the babies abandoned in hospitals and nurseries, in doctors' offices and on strangers' laps, on park benches and in garbage cans, the chilled, the urine-soaked, the withered babies left choking under pillows, rescued from gas-filled rooms crushed against the wall, thrown on the ground, abandoned amid broken glass and potato peelings; let them all come, our unbidden avenging enemies.

> ... let all the others come, those whom no amount of candy, tears, and toy trains can keep at home, who climb out of the window, toss their school bags into the cellar, hide stolen money under their inner soles, arm themselves with compass, kitchen knife, paper mask, and flashlight, and set out for the border, for new worlds across the sea, but end up in jail.

> ... let the tyrants of selfishness come, with all their manias and deadly, futile wrongs; those who rage on the telephone because they

can't get through, those who wallow in excuses, the secret judges
who can never acquit themselves, the martyrs who ultimately die of
some comic misunderstanding, the leeches and hamsters of love,
the shivering outcasts, the lepers whose birthday no one remembers,
those who when embraced in front feel lonely behind, whose bright
new penny always gets stolen by a magpie.

...let the eternal underdogs come, those whose ribs are crushed
year in year out by the same steel spring, whom conjugal love alone
prevents from stretching their legs, who have never had as much
room as a convict in a humane prison system, who hold their breath
when they copulate, who through their cellar windows see only the
shoes of their fellow creatures, who are never alone except in their
fourth-rate coffins, those around whom iron turns to rust, plaster
crumbles, wood rots, cloth grows threadbare, the window mists
over and cracks.

...the neglected who have never been given anything for nothing,
the underprivileged whose wildest dream it is to be the next to last,
those who live with their backs to the wall, always looking for a
place to hide, cringing before they are threatened, those who cannot
even be sure their mother will recognize them tomorrow, those who
shuffle from one foot to the other and finally decide not to ring the
bell after all.

...let all those come who want to; one of us will talk, the other will
listen; at least we shall be together.

References

Chapter 1: What is social work?

Australian Human Rights Commission (1997) *Bringing Them Home: The 'Stolen Children' Report*, <https://www.humanrights.gov.au/publications/bringing-them-home-stolen-children-report-1997> accessed January 2015.

Barber, J. (2002) *Social Work with Addictions*, 2nd edition, Basingstoke, Palgrave.

Barclay Report (1982) *Social Workers: Their Roles and Tasks*, London, Bedford Street Press/National Council for Voluntary Organisations.

Bartlett, H. (1958) 'Working Definition of Social Work Practice', *Social Work* 3 (2): 5–8.

International Federation of Social Workers and International Association of Schools of Social Work (2014) 'Global Definition of Social Work', <http://ifsw.org/get-involved/global-definition-of-social-work/> accessed January 2015.

Payne, M. (2005) *The Origins of Social Work*, Basingstoke, Palgrave.

Rogers, C. (1957) 'The Necessary and Sufficient Conditions of Therapeutic Personality Change', *Journal of Consulting Psychology* 21 (2): 95–103.

Truell, R. (2014) 'What Is Social Work?' *The Guardian* social care network, 7 July, <http://www.theguardian.com/social-care-network/2014/jul/07/what-is-social-work> accessed January 2015.

Chapter 2: The politics of social work

Butler, I. and Drakeford, M. (2005) *Scandal, Social Policy and Social Welfare*, 2nd edition, Bristol, Policy Press.

Esping-Andersen, G. (1990) *The Three Worlds of Welfare Capitalism*, Cambridge, Polity.

Halmos, P. (1967) 'The Personal Service Society', *The British Journal of Sociology* 18: 13–28.

Howe, D. (1987) *An Introduction to Social Work Theory*, Aldershot, Wildwood House.

Payne, M. (2006) *What Is Professional Social Work?*, 2nd edition, Bristol, Policy Press.

Schur, E. (1973) *Radical Non-Intervention: Rethinking the Delinquency Problem*, Englewood Cliffs, NJ, Prentice-Hall.

Shakespeare, T. (2014) *Disability Rights and Wrongs Revisited*, Abingdon and New York, Routledge.

Chapter 3: Social work with individuals and families

Ainsworth, M., Blehar, M., Waters, E., and Wall, S. (1978) *Patterns of Attachment*, Hillsdale, NJ, Erlbaum Associates.

AASW (2012) *Social Work and Mental Health Position Paper*, Australian Association of Social Workers, <http://www.aasw.asn.au/document/item/3284> accessed January 2015.

Bowlby, J. (1969) *Attachment and Loss, Vol. 1: Attachment*, New York, Basic Books.

Bronfenbrenner, U. (1979) *The Ecology of Human Development*, Cambridge, MA, Harvard University Press.

Caplan, G. (1964) *Principles of Preventive Psychiatry*, New York, Basic Books.

Hollis, F. (1964) *Casework: A Psychosocial Therapy*, New York, Random House.

Lindemann, E. (1944) 'Symptomatology and Management of Acute Grief', *American Journal of Psychiatry* 101: 141–8.

Mayer, J. E. and Timms, N. (1970) *The Client Speaks*, London, Routledge and Kegan Paul.

Miller, W. R. and Rollnick, S. (1991) *Motivational Interviewing: Preparing People to Change Addictive Behavior*, New York, Guilford Press.

NASW (2013) *NASW Standards for Case Management*, National Association of Social Workers, <http://www.socialworkers.org/practice/naswstandards/CaseManagementStandards2013.pdf> accessed January 2015.

Prochaska, J. and DiClemente, C. (1983) 'Stages and Processes of Self-Change in Smoking: Toward an Integrative Model of Change', *Journal of Consulting and Clinical Psychology* 5: 390–5.

Reid, W. and Epstein, L. (1972) *Task-Centred Casework*, London, Columbia University Press.

Richmond, M. (1917) *Social Diagnosis*, New York, Russell Sage Foundation.

Rogers, C. (1961) *On Becoming a Person*, Boston, Houghton Mifflin.

Chapter 4: Social work with groups

Bowlby, J. (1951) *Maternal Care and Mental Health*, New York, Schocken.

Butler, I. and Drakeford, M. (2012) *Social Work on Trial: The Colwell Inquiry and the State of Welfare*, Bristol, Policy Press.

Goffman, E. (1961) *Asylums: Essays on the Social Situation of Mental Patients and Other Inmates*, New York, Doubleday Anchor.

Higginbotham, P. (2014) 'The Workhouse in Scotland', <http://www.workhouses.org.uk/Scotland/> accessed January 2015.

Lewin, K. (1947) 'Frontiers in Group Dynamics: II. Channels of Group Life; Social Planning and Action Research', *Human Relations* 1: 143–53.

Seebohm, F. (1968) *Report of the Committee on Local Authority and Allied Social Services*, London, HMSO.

Tuckman, B. (1965) 'Developmental Sequence in Small Groups', *Psychological Bulletin* 63: 384–99.

Chapter 5: Community social work

Barclay, P. (1982) *Social Workers: Their Role and Tasks*, The Barclay Report, London, Bedford Square Press.

Burrows, R. (1905) 'The Dragon', in B. M. Bull (1965) *The University Settlement in Cardiff*, pamphlet produced in The School of Printing, Cardiff College of Art.

Calouste Gulbenkian Foundation (1968) *Community Work and Social Change: A Report on Training*, London, Longman.

Dickens, J. and Groza, V. (2004) 'Empowerment in Difficulty: A Critical Appraisal of International Intervention in Child Welfare in Romania', *International Social Work* 47 (4): 469–87.

Family Action in Rogerfield and Easterhouse <http://www.fare-scotland.org/> accessed January 2015.

Freire, P. (1970) *Pedagogy of the Oppressed*, New York, Continuum.

Integrated Village Development Project (IVDP) <http://www.ivdpkrishnagiri.org/index.php> accessed January 2015.

Jordan, B. (2000) *Social Work and the Third Way: Tough Love As Social Policy*, London, Sage.

Seebohm, F. (chair) (1968) *Report of the Committee on Local Authority and Allied Social Services*, London, HMSO.

Chapter 6: Does it work and how do we know?

England, H. (1986) *Social Work As Art: Making Sense for Good Practice*, London, Allen and Unwin.

Konrád, G. (1987) *The Case Worker*, New York, Viking Penguin.

McCord, J. (1978) 'A Thirty-Year Follow-Up of Treatment Effects', *American Psychologist* 33 (3): 284–9.

Mullen, E. J. and Shuluk, J. (2011) 'Outcomes of Social Work Intervention in the Context of Evidence-Based Practice', *Journal of Social Work* 11 (1): 49–63.

Pawson, R. and Tilley, N. (1997) *Realistic Evaluation*, London, Sage.

Petrosino, A., Turpin-Petrosino, C., Hollis-Peel, M. E., and Lavenberg, J. G. (2013) '"Scared Straight" and Other Juvenile Awareness Programs for Preventing Juvenile Delinquency', *Cochrane Database of Systematic Reviews* 4: CD002796.

Reid, W. J. (1997) 'Evaluating the Dodo's Verdict: Do All Interventions Have Equivalent Outcomes?' *Social Work Research* 21 (1): 5–16.

Sheldon, B. and Macdonald, G. (2009) *A Textbook of Social Work*, London, Routledge.

White, S., Wastell, D., Broadhurst, K., and Hall, C. (2010) 'When Policy O'erleaps Itself: The "Tragic Tale" of the Integrated Children's System', *Critical Social Policy* 30: 405–29.

Winokur, M., Holtan, A., and Batchelder, K. E. (2014) 'Kinship Care for the Safety, Permanency, and Well-Being of Children Removed from the Home for Maltreatment: A Systematic Review', *Campbell Systematic Reviews* 2.

You, E. C., Dunt, D., Doyle, C., and Hsueh, A. (2012) 'Effects of Case Management in Community Aged Care on Client and Carer Outcomes: A Systematic Review of Randomized Trials and Comparative Observational Studies', *BMC Health Services Research* 12: 395.

Further reading

What is social work?

Banks, S. (2012) *Ethics and Values in Social Work*, 4th edition, Basingstoke, Palgrave. A very useful introduction to professional ethics.

Dominelli, L. (2003) *Anti-Oppressive Social Work Theory and Practice*, Basingstoke, Palgrave. A strong statement of social work's role in combatting discrimination and oppression.

Gray, M., Coates, J., and Yellow Bird, M. (eds) (2008) *Indigenous Social Work Around the World: Towards Culturally Relevant Education and Practice*, Burlington, VT, Ashgate. There are contributions in this book from social workers from a range of cultural backgrounds including China, Tonga, Botswana, Malaysia, and indigenous people of the Americas, Australia, and New Zealand. The book overall provides an important criticism of the imperial nature of Western social work theories and practices.

Healy, L. (2008) *International Social Work*, 2nd edition, New York, Oxford University Press. This gives a flavour of the international variation in manifestations of social work.

Hugman, R. (2009) 'But Is it Social Work? Some Reflections on Mistaken Identities', *British Journal of Social Work* 39 (6): 1138–53. This article is a good place to start in tracing the divergent traditions of individual and community work from social work's history to the present.

Lavalette, M. (ed.) (2011) *Radical Social Work Today*, Bristol, Policy Press. A recent collection of writings in the radical social work tradition, which has been somewhat revived in recent years in the

UK via the Social Work Action Network <http://www.social
workfuture.org/> accessed January 2015.

Payne, M. (2006) *What Is Professional Social Work?*, 2nd edition,
Bristol, Policy Press. An overview of debates about social work's
purpose and professional identity.

A special issue of the journal *Research on Social Work Practice* published
in 2003 (issue 13, number 3), is dedicated to a debate on Bartlett's
definition of social work practice and its contemporary relevance.

History

History of Social Work is a more internationally orientated social work
history website, which provides interesting profiles of key figures,
quizzes, and recommended reading. There are also Dutch and
Flemish versions <http://historyofsocialwork.org/eng/index.php>
accessed January 2015.

Nigel Parton is a British academic who has, over thirty years, traced
the politics of child abuse in masterly fashion, locating government
policies in their wider social and political context. Every few years
he has updated his analysis. Any of his books are worth a read. The
most recent, published in 2014, is *The Politics of Child Protection:
Contemporary Developments and Future Directions*, Basingstoke,
Palgrave Macmillan.

Payne, M. (2005) *The Origins of Social Work*, Basingstoke, Palgrave.
An overview of social work's history, which focuses on Britain and
the US but also has a reasonably international scope.

The Social Welfare History Project website is a treasure trove of
photographs, documents, and accounts of key people, movements,
and policies in the history of social welfare, including many social
work pioneers. It mainly covers American social work history.
<http://www.socialwelfarehistory.com/> accessed January 2015.

Social work practices

Healy, K. (2005) *Social Work in Context: Creating Frameworks for
Practice*, Basingstoke, Palgrave. This provides a useful and
accessible overview of the theoretical underpinnings of social work
practice, particularly its psychological and sociological roots.

Midgley, J. (2014) *Social Development: Theory and Practice*, London,
Sage. This is the latest of several important texts on the subject by

this author. This book combines theories of social development with lots of case examples from around the world.

Parton, N. and O'Byrne, P. (2000) *Constructive Social Work*, Basingstoke, Macmillan, marks a shift of emphasis from social worker-as-expert to social worker-as-listener and collaborator with individuals and families. It is part of a 'narrative turn' in social work theory and practice in the 21st century.

Sheldon, B. and Macdonald, G. (2009) *A Textbook of Social Work*, London, Routledge. This elegantly written book provides an overview of social work past and present, with a strong emphasis on practice models which are evidence-based.

Stepney, P. and Popple, K. (2008) *Social Work and the Community*, Basingstoke, Palgrave Macmillan. This book examines the concept of community, the contribution of classic community studies, community social policies, theories, and practices.

Ward, A. (2007) *Working in Group Care*, 2nd edition, Bristol, Policy Press. This book provides an accessible overview of residential and day care services. It provides practical tips on how these services work best, but also draws on research and theory to inform these.

Useful websites

The Campbell Collaboration <http://www.campbellcollaboration.org/> is a repository of systematic reviews in education, crime and justice, social welfare, and international development.

There are also some systematic reviews relevant to social work in the portfolio of the more well-established and more health-oriented Cochrane Collaboration <http://www.cochrane.org/>. 0002481009.

The 'Information for Practice' website <http://ifp.nyu.edu/> is maintained by Prof. Gary Holden from New York University, who has been providing a guide to the World Wide Web for social workers since the mid-1990s.

The website for the British *Social Care Institute for Excellence* <http://www.scie.org.uk/> provides an introduction to all types of social work, information for practitioners, and reviews of evidence.

Index

SOCIAL MEDIA
Very Short Introduction

Join our community
www.oup.com/vsi

- Join us online at the official Very Short Introductions **Facebook** page.
- Access the thoughts and musings of our authors with our online **blog**.
- Sign up for our monthly **e-newsletter** to receive information on all new titles publishing that month.
- Browse the full range of Very Short Introductions online.
- Read **extracts** from the Introductions for free.
- Visit our library of **Reading Guides**. These guides, written by our expert authors will help you to question again, why you think what you think.
- If you are a teacher or lecturer you can order inspection copies quickly and simply via our website.